THE REAL READER'S QUARTERLY

Slightly Foxed

'Mellow Fruitfulness'

D0543975

NO.40   WINTER 2013

Editors Gail Pirkis and Hazel Wood
Marketing and publicity Stephanie Allen and Jennie Paterson
Subscriptions Alarys Gibson, Anna Kirk and Faith McAllister

Cover illustration: Christopher Corr, 'Now We Are Ten'

Christopher Corr's painting is inspired by his travels around the globe. Vivid colours and city scenes are what excite him. Recent commissions include a series of portraits of the Shard for the Shard, paintings about fish for the restaurant Kensington Place in Notting Hill and book illustrations for the Folio Society and Andersen Press. More examples of his work can be seen at www.christophercorr.com and www.rowleygallery.com.

Design by Octavius Murray

Layout by Andrew Evans

Colophon and tailpiece by David Eccles

© The contributors 2013

Published by Slightly Foxed Limited
53 Hoxton Square
London N1 6PB

tel 020 7033 0258
fax 0870 1991245
e-mail all@foxedquarterly.com
www.foxedquarterly.com

Slightly Foxed is published quarterly in early March, June, September and December
Annual subscription rates (4 issues)
UK £40; Europe £48; Rest of the World £52
Single copies of this issue can be bought for £10 (UK), £12 (Europe) or £13 (Rest of the World)
Back issues are also available

ISBN 978-1-906562-57-1

Printed and bound by Smith Settle, Yeadon, West Yorkshire

Contents

Contents

F. W. Marston, 'Shooting star'

Our bookshop can obtain any of the books mentioned in this issue.
Slightly Foxed on Gloucester Road, 123 Gloucester Road,
London SW7 4TE · enquiries@foxedbooks.com · tel 020 7370 3503

From the Editors

This fortieth issue is a very special one for us. It marks the beginning of our anniversary year – ten years since we came up with the idea for *Slightly Foxed* and tentatively put together our first issue. They're years in which we've got to know some of the most likeable and entertaining people – both subscribers and contributors – enjoyed some of the best laughs, been introduced to some of the best books, and had some of the most varied (and sometimes eccentric) experiences. During those years children have married and grand-children have been born, *Slightly Foxed* has grown, and we've been joined by some exceptionally nice, clever and hardworking young members of staff. We can only say thank you to the Fox and to all of you who've supported us for giving us some of the happiest years of our working lives.

Of course we're going to celebrate – first of all with a party in Bloomsbury on 24 February. We wish we could invite you all, but that would be a cast of thousands, so instead we'll be offering ten tickets, each of which will admit one subscriber and a guest. The successful names will be drawn out of a hat on 14 January. If you'd like to be included in the draw, do give us a ring. We also wanted to mark the anniversary in a way that would help a good cause, so in the spring we'll be publishing a very unusual little book to raise money for a charity which is close to our hearts. We won't say more now but will give you the details in March when it's available.

Another good cause certainly worth supporting is cancer research. This year a group of distinguished actors including Judi Dench, Anthony Hopkins, Sam West and Penelope Wilton have got together to raise funds for Cancer Research UK – which depends entirely on donations to carry out its work – with a CD called *Given for Christmas*. Recorded in St Paul's and Westminster Cathedrals, it includes Christmas readings of poetry and prose, both religious and secular. It's available from the Slightly Foxed bookshop (020 7370 3503, www.foxedbooks.com) and costs £9.99.

As Christmas approaches it's all go in the office here with gift orders and subscriptions, and Jennie, Anna, Faith, Aimi (who comes in from the shop once a week to do the accounts), Chudleigh and the rest of us are dodging round a positive fortress of heavy brown paper parcels in the middle of the floor. These contain the first three Slightly Foxed Cubs – *Knight Crusader*, *The Galleon* and *For the King* – and Gwen Raverat's *Period Piece*, the latest of the Slightly Foxed Editions. This enchanting account of growing up in Victorian Cambridge at the heart of the large and idiosyncratic Darwin clan must be one of the best-loved books in the English language, and it's hard to think of anyone with an interest in people and a sense of humour who wouldn't enjoy it. Details of *Period Piece* and all our other publications are included in the leaflet slipped into this issue, as is our fifth literary crossword.

And finally, a cheering thought. Recently *The Times* reported research which showed that 'people who engage in mentally stimulating activity such as reading, or even visiting libraries at any point in their life', have a slower rate of decline when they reach old age. Perhaps common sense might have told us this already, but it's good to know that it's now official. The new up-to-date Index to *Slightly Foxed* included with this issue is a reminder, if one is needed, that there are plenty of good books and interesting writers still left to read. It comes with our very best wishes for a peaceful Christmas and a more optimistic New Year.

GAIL PIRKIS
HAZEL WOOD

Now we are ten: Posy Simmonds raises a glass

Mellow Fruitfulness

MELISSA HARRISON

What do we lose when we become a nation of urbanites? A connection to nature, sometimes – though not necessarily. An awareness of the seasons, an understanding of the farming year; a sense of community, perhaps, and of being bound to a particular spot by ties of history and blood.

Gathered from his long-running weekly column in the *Church Times*, Ronald Blythe's Wormingford books are an evocation of village life that, as a city-dweller, I find deeply comforting. To say that is to risk making his lovely miniatures sound twee or nostalgic, when in fact they are pragmatic about the changes that are happening in our countryside; what they offer, though, is a vision of life that has deep meaning, meaning created quite effortlessly from art and literature, the natural world and the kinship of neighbours.

Of course, given their provenance, these short pieces are also about faith. Blythe is a lay reader in the benefice of Wormingford and Mount Bures with Little Horkesley – the Church of England parish in which his Wormingford books are set – and his awareness of the religious calendar and knowledge of the Scriptures suffuse each piece. I am an atheist – albeit one who was brought up attending a village church not too dissimilar to the ones he describes – but I love his writing not in spite of its religious content but because of it: for the

---

Ronald Blythe, *Word from Wormingford* (1998), *The Circling Year* (2001), *A Year at Bottengoms Farm* (2007), *The Bookman's Tale* (2009) and *Village Hours* (2012) are all available as paperbacks from the Canterbury Press in Norwich: tel 01603 785900, www.canterburypress.co.uk.

way in which belief is woven with gossip, local history, nature writing and gentle irony to create a picture of faith that is personal and idiosyncratic yet connected to an English tradition that spans the centuries – and which, whether or not we believe in God, belongs to all of us.

John Nash

Blythe has lived his life in the company of artists and writers, from Cedric Morris to Patricia Highsmith. As a young man working as a librarian in Colchester he became friends with the painter John Nash and his wife Christine, often visiting them at Bottengoms Farm, which Nash would later bequeath him and in which he still lives today: an ancient yeoman's house at the end of a narrow track, fed by a spring and surrounded by trees.

The Nashes encouraged him to write, and over the years that followed he spent time with E. M. Forster, edited the Aldeburgh

Festival programmes for Benjamin Britten and began to produce fiction, poetry and essays. Along the way he published *Akenfield* (see *SF* No. 11), the book for which he's best known, a collection of oral histories documenting the voices of the last generation to work the land; it was made into a film by Peter Hall. He's written over thirty books and edited many more.

Now in his tenth decade, Blythe remains astonishingly prolific. A book about his friendship with Britten, called *The Time by the Sea: Aldeburgh 1955–1958*, was published in June, and as well as reviews, articles and forewords he still writes the hugely popular weekly column from which *Word from Wormingford*, *A Year at Bottengoms Farm*, *Village Hours*, *The Bookman's Tale*, *The Circling Year* and the other Wormingford books are taken.

His fruitfulness is hardly surprising, though. These short essays reveal him to have a vast curiosity about the world, from modern agricultural methods to the inner lives of his neighbours, and from landscape history to the adventures of his white cat – and he is someone for whom, one feels, thinking and writing are the same thing. In fact, one of the ways in which these pieces are unique is the sense they give of following a thought quite naturally as it darts here and there, starting with (for example) the words of a hymn before touching on a childhood memory, taking in a literary reference and ending with a natural observation – yet all tied together so elegantly that reading each one is like exploring an origami sculpture of beautifully folded prose.

'"O, go to Jericho" mother would say when we exasperated her,' opens a piece entitled 'Trinity Six' in *Word from Wormingford*. It goes on to describe the baked brownness of the Holy Land, comparing it to English barley fields in mid-July and recalling the texture of the crop on bare, childhood legs; from there to the crops growing locally that year ('"Why are you growing borage, Hugh?" "For Pimm's Number One"') and the current crop of (probably brown) signs on village verges directing summer traffic to local attractions, before making quiet reference to Philip Larkin's poem 'Here' and ending with 'I do not wish to be entertained. I am in a brown study.' It seems effortless, but to control such generous material so elegantly requires a lightness of touch and a level of control that together are breathtaking.

Blythe's curiosity about the world also results in an appealing sense of democracy: everything is interesting, everything is worthy of investigation. It makes him childlike – not childish, but with the eager inquisitiveness that most of us, sadly, lose as we get older. And because he doesn't presume to understand everything about the world, very little attracts his censure, because understanding must come before judgement. This humility makes him extremely likeable:

> I am waiting for a bus which I caught when I was a child . . . once the conductor would shout, 'Chapel Corner!' when it arrived where I am standing in the cold spring rain. Instead of contemplating Duncan's flat field and the little cottage which was once the lemonade shop (a spoonful of yellow crystals in half a pint of water for a penny) I find myself counting the things a village bus stop must have, the latest being the elevation of the timetable from four drawing pins in the shelter to a fine steel frame on a pole. Nothing is too good for a timetable. Drawing pins are now reduced to supporting our flower festival notice and a picture of a fat lady who has slimmed.
> ('Maundy Thursday', *A Year at Bottengoms Farm*)

Unlike many writers only half as erudite Blythe never seems pompous, always taking care to bring a literary reference back down to earth and neatly tying it to the subject in hand. Nevertheless, he is fearsomely well read, from George Herbert and John Clare to Traherne, the Metaphysical poets, obscure diarists and, of course, the Bible, which in his hands becomes a luminously accessible book of stories that weave in and out of daily life. On the village's annual Rogation walk he reflects,

Back to our asking journey among the crops . . . 'Ask for the old paths, the good way,' implores Jeremiah of half-lost Israel. The Lord is reproachful: 'So far you have asked nothing in my name: ask and you shall receive.' Our farm and field asking lacks the old intensity. Local agriculture supplies but a fraction of the local needs. And there is always Sainsbury's . . .

('Rogation Two', *Word from Wormingford*)

His use of the first-person plural is characteristic, speaking, as he often does, for the congregation, and the village, of which he is a part. And these are people for whom he cares deeply, and in whom he finds wisdom and goodness: 'I had an old farmworker friend who read the Lesson. When it carried him away, as it often did, he would pause, then say, "That was very fine. I'll read that agen' " . . . he would have been perplexed had he known that I still hear him in my head as one of the oracles of God.'

John Nash

When I think of the Wormingford books, what springs to mind even more than their lovely evocation of a faith I don't share is the picture they paint of the English countryside that, as an urbanite, I miss. Bottengoms Farm is surrounded by a rambling garden in which cow parsley, white nettles and other 'undesirables' thrive alongside roses and runner beans. It is enfolded by trees, and beyond those lie fields of wheat, barley and the 'bright parallelograms' of rape. It is Gainsborough and Constable country – and Nash country, of course – and Blythe's descriptions of the sowing and harvesting, the weather and the seasons are little masterpieces, almost pointillist in their detail and clarity: 'Jean's horses run on the hillside in praise of February, chasing and wheeling in the afternoon light, their manes flung out like flags.'

He can recall the last of the farm horses, and for him the land in which he is rooted now seems strangely quiet and unpeopled – 'Modern farming has brought about such a desertion of the field that the sight of John on the harrow and Peter's men at work on a vast onion bed halts one in one's tracks. "Look! People!"' Yet he is not sentimental, having a clearer understanding than most of what hard toil a life on the land really was. Of the ancient ash tree by the house he writes, 'Alone of all the still living witnesses to the purpose of Bottengoms it seems to have, in its writhing roots and broken tips, a notion of what it was like to let the fields take all your strength.'

Blythe's is not an unchanging landscape, but it is given deep meaning by history; and the village life he describes so lovingly, with its commuters, quiet fields and half-full churches, is in his hands as spiritually rich as Little Gidding – or Gethsemane. Even for an unbeliever like me.

MELISSA HARRISON is the author of *Clay*, a nature novel set in a British city (www.claynovel.com). She lives in South London.

Cambridge Canvas

HAZEL WOOD

For almost a decade there's been one particular book we've been long-ing to reissue. Now at last, as we reach our tenth anniversary, we've got the opportunity to do so. When I wrote about it in one of our very early issues, I said that for me a home without a copy of Gwen Raverat's *Period Piece* (1952) was like a home without a cat – lacking an essential cheering and comfortable element – and for me that still holds true.

In fact I've got several copies – the original dignified, well-produced pink Faber paperback, the infinitely inferior paperback they replaced it with, and now the lovely little Slightly Foxed hard-back edition. It's the kind of book that cries out to be read in a nice edition. Gwen Raverat was an artist after all, very particular about the look of things and about the placing of her illustrations, which provide a delicious counterpoint to the text. Looking at our edition I think she would have been pleased.

She was also, on the showing of *Period Piece*, a brilliant writer, with that well-tuned ear and perfect judgement that makes an an-ecdote funny, and the affectionate observation that brings her characters alive. It's true that the book can be quite an irritation for other people because one is tempted to interrupt them all the time by reading bits aloud, but as far as I'm concerned that is its only defect.

Period Piece is Gwen's account of growing up in academic Cambridge in the last years of the nineteenth century. 'This is a cir-cular book,' she writes in a preface. 'It does not begin at the beginning and go on to the end; it is all going on at the same time, sticking out like the spokes of a wheel from the hub, which is me. So it does not matter which chapter is read first or last.' There is no 'storyline', but the individual chapters gradually build into a complete picture, like a mosaic. Open the book at any point and you are plunged straight into the atmosphere of Victorian Cambridge and some new and probably highly entertaining aspect of Gwen's childhood.

It was a safe, warm, gas-lit world bounded by the limits of Gwen's large and eccentric extended family, the Darwins – her paternal grandfather was Charles Darwin and her father, George Darwin, was a Fellow of Trinity College and eventually the University's Plumian Professor of Astronomy. The family contained numerous Fellows of the Royal Society as well as a good sprinkling of artists, poets and musicians, including George's cousin, the composer Ralph Vaughan Williams.

Two of George's four brothers – Frank and Horace – had built family houses in the spacious meadows next to a house called The Grove in Huntingdon Road where their mother, Charles Darwin's widow, and her unmarried daughter Aunt Bessy spent their winters. So Gwen and her brothers and sister grew up with a ready supply of entertaining and affectionate aunts, uncles and cousins, including Gwen's special friend Frances, who would become known as a poet under her married name of Cornford.

Two mortals could hardly have been more different than Gwen's lively, sociable American mother Maud and her quiet intellectual father, but fortunately they seem to have complemented rather than irritated one another. They had fallen in love when Maud was visiting her glamorous Aunt Cara, wife of the future Professor of Greek at the university, Richard Jebb, and the two had married in 1884. They settled at Newnham Grange, an old mill house on the Backs, which was romantic though damp, and in the early days, when all Cambridge's sewage still drained into the river, distinctly smelly. (It's said that when Queen Victoria was being shown over Trinity College by the Master, Dr Whewell, she was curious to know what all the pieces of paper floating down the river were, to which, with great presence of mind, he replied, 'Those, ma'am, are notices that bathing is forbidden.')

Like all the Darwins George was something of a hypochondriac, but fortunately marriage to Maud had a comforting effect. 'My mother's calmness, good spirits and unshakeable courage were very soothing to my father's over-strung nerves,' observes Gwen. 'She was always kind and sympathetic to him when he was ill, and took his ailments perfectly seriously; but unlike a Darwin she did not positively enjoy his ill-health . . . and as a consequence he did get very much better.'

This was in sharp contrast to Gwen's much-loved Aunt Etty who, after having a 'low fever' at the age of 13, had been recommended by the doctor to have breakfast in bed for a time and *never got up for breakfast again.* When there were colds about she would put on a protective mask of her own invention, made from a wire kitchen strainer stuffed with antiseptic cotton-wool and tied on like a snout, from behind which she would discuss politics in a hollow voice, oblivious of the fact that visitors were struggling with fits of laughter.

Childless Aunt Etty, like many Victorian women, had few outlets for her abundant energy, so a great deal of it was concentrated on the health of her husband, Uncle Richard. Poor Uncle Richard, it seems, had not originally been ill, but Aunt Etty had decided that he was extremely delicate 'and he was very obliging about it', eating up his doses of Benger's Food (known to the children in the family as 'Uncle Richard's porridge') like a man. And 'if a window had to be opened to air the room in cold weather, Aunt Etty covered him up entirely with a dust sheet for fear of draughts; and he sat there as patient as a statue, till he could be unveiled.'

Gwen's mother Maud may have been calm, but she was also somewhat happy-go-lucky and inclined to leave the finer points of organization to others. There is a description of her preparing to leave for a day's shopping in London, or even for the boat train to

New York, still in her nightdress but perfectly composed as the horse-drawn cab with 'red-faced old Ellis' on the box waits outside to take her to the station, and the three maids rush hither and thither. 'Of course she had not attempted breakfast,' writes Gwen, 'and I used to put slices of buttered toast on the seat of the cab for her.'

When the family went on holiday to a rented house in Yorkshire, it was Gwen's father who organized the 'awful journey', with changes at Ely and York and a caravan of luggage and maids and dogs, and Nana and the pram and the parrot and the cot and the bath for the children. Maud would arrive comfortably a few days later to find them nicely settled in. 'We enjoyed doing it, and we did it perfectly well, so all was for the best. But most mothers would have thought it their duty to do more of the fussing themselves.'

Maud's views on the upbringing of children were refreshingly modern for she had a sturdy American belief in independence. They were encouraged to do things for themselves, unlike the well-brought-up English children of their class, 'some of whom simply did not know that you *could* make a bed yourself'. Gwen was only once spanked – when she amused herself during an enforced afternoon rest on her mother's bed by drawing on the white wallpaper with a red lip-salve. 'Now resting is a foolish theory, from which many parents suffer,' she writes.

> It is far too exhausting for children, it is really only suitable for the old. I used to get absolutely worn out inventing games to play during the ages when I was condemned to 'rest'; so that by the time the rest was over, I really did need a rest.

Despite Maud's relaxed approach, certain activities were nonetheless *de rigueur*. 'The first religious experience I can remember', writes Gwen, 'is getting under the nursery table to pray that the dancing mistress might be dead before we got to the dancing class.'

As well as being one of the funniest memoirs I've read, *Period Piece*

Gwen's dreaded dancing class . . .

is also one of the most magical, especially in its descriptions of the summers the family spent at Down House in Kent, home of Gwen's paternal grandmother, a Wedgwood by birth (Darwins had married Wedgwoods in two successive generations) and widow of Charles who had died in 1882, three years before Gwen was born.

To Gwen and the rest of the family Down was paradise and perfection. George and his brothers had all grown up there and would never hear a word against the place. Uncle Horace was once heard to say in a surprised voice, 'No, I don't like salvias very much, *though they did grow at Down.*' 'Of course,' writes Gwen, 'all the flowers that grew at Down were beautiful; and different from all other flowers. Everything there was different. And better.'

Perhaps, she hazards, life there had in some ways been a little too perfect. The whole family was known for its love of children and animals – Gwen's great-grandfather, Josiah Wedgwood II (1769–1843), had had some quite startlingly liberal views on the upbringing of

'. . . I have just been sent out of the room in disgrace'

children, and Charles Darwin himself was such a tolerant and broad-
minded father that his sons had never had to rebel. The result was
that they 'seemed never quite to get away from that early Elysium, or
quite to belong to the ordinary horrid world'.

Gwen's own feelings about Down were quite literally ones of
adoration:

It was adoration I felt for the foxgloves at Down . . . and for the
beautiful white paint on the nursery floor. This kind of feeling
hits you in the stomach, and in the ends of your fingers, and it
is probably the most important thing in life. Long after I have
forgotten all my human loves, I shall remember the smell of a
gooseberry leaf, or the feel of the wet grass on my bare feet; or
the pebbles in the path. In the long run it is this feeling that
makes life worth living, this which is the driving force behind
the artist's need to create.

Gwen did of course become an artist, and her wood engravings (which Simon Brett discussed in *Slightly Foxed*, No. 9) communicate just this feeling of joy and ecstatic connection with the natural world. They are wonderful things, but in *Period Piece* she created a different and equally lasting kind of small masterpiece, which reads as freshly now as it did when I first opened it more than forty years ago.

HAZEL WOOD has always worked with words, but sometimes wishes she could have been an artist.

Gwen Raverat's *Period Piece* (320pp) is now available from *Slightly Foxed* in a new limited and numbered cloth-bound pocket edition of 2,000 copies, each priced at £13.50 (plus p&p: UK £2.50, Europe £4.50, Rest of the World £5.50). Copies may be ordered by post, by phone (020 7033 0258) or via our website www.foxedquarterly.com.

The following Slightly Foxed Editions are also still available:

Ted Walker, *The High Path*
Graham Greene, *A Sort of Life*
P. Y. Betts, *People Who Say Goodbye*
Frances Wood, *Hand-grenade Practice in Peking*
Dodie Smith, *Look Back with Love*
Suzanne St Albans, *Mango and Mimosa*
Elspeth Huxley, *The Flame Trees of Thika*
Alan Moorehead, *A Late Education*
Denis Constanduros, *My Grandfather & Father, Dear Father*
Ysenda Maxtone Graham, *The Real Mrs Miniver*
Richard Hillyer, *Country Boy*
Christabel Bielenberg, *The Past Is Myself*

The Passing of Old Europe

C. J. SCHÜLER

It was a passing reference in Robert Musil's novel *The Man without Qualities* to 'the oracular casting of lead that fate performs with us' that jogged my memory. When I was a child, on New Year's Eve, we would melt small lead ingots in a spoon over a candle flame, and drop the silvery liquid into a jug of water. The shape it assumed as it fell, hissing and steaming into the future, was said to predict what the coming year held in store. It is an old German tradition that my father, a refugee from the Third Reich, upheld.

I first read this great and mysterious classic of European literature in my twenties, seeking to understand more about my own Central European heritage. At the time, the only English translation available was the original 1950s version by Eithne Wilkins and Ernst Kaiser, published by Secker and Warburg and reissued by Picador in three paperback volumes with edgy, Expressionist portraits by Egon Schiele on the covers. I was immediately transfixed.

The year is 1913. Ulrich, a former cavalry officer who has tried to make a career as a civil engineer and mathematician, returns to Vienna from his travels to take 'a year out from his life' while he decides what to do next. He embarks on desultory affairs with a nightclub *chanteuse* and a married woman who rescues him after a mugging, and becomes emotionally entangled with Clarisse, the highly strung wife of his artistic friend Walter, unwittingly opening a

Robert Musil, *The Man without Qualities* (1930–43) · Trans. Sophie Wilkins and Burton Pike
Picador · Pb · 1,130pp · £16.99 · ISBN 9781447211877

secret empty room in her psyche 'where something tore at chains that might some day rend apart'.

The city in which the action takes place is not the picturesque old Vienna of Baroque churches and pastry shops, but a maelstrom of modernism. From his home in an old hunting lodge, now engulfed by the expanding metropolis, Ulrich looks out on to a violet-blue haze of petrol hanging over the tarmacked streets. Like Andrei Bely's almost contemporary novel *Petersburg*, *The Man without Qualities* presents an imperial capital ablaze with neon advertising, gridlocked with motor cars and fizzing with dangerous new ideas. This is the Vienna of Freud, Mahler, Schoenberg, Klimt, Schrödinger, Schumpeter, Wittgenstein . . . and Musil. It is the capital of the state that sparked the conflict that would define the course of the twentieth century.

In a prison cell, awaiting judgement, sits Ulrich's Jungian shadow: the startlingly modern figure of the sex-murderer Moosbrugger, with whom Clarisse is obsessed. An itinerant carpenter whose benign appearance belies his psychopathic crimes, this articulate autodidact has developed an elaborate theoretical justification of his actions. Like Ulrich, he considers himself beyond good and evil (Nietzsche lies just below the surface of the novel), and in that respect both embody their age. The gruesome details of his crimes send a shame-fully pleasurable frisson through the newspaper-reading public. 'If mankind could dream collectively,' Ulrich thinks, 'it would dream Moosbrugger.'

Milan Kundera has described Musil, along with Kafka, Hermann Broch, Jaroslaw Hašek and Witold Gombrowicz, as one of 'the pleiad of great Central European novelists'. *The Man without Qualities* also belongs to a select group of novels, including Thomas Mann's *The Magic Mountain*, Broch's *The Sleepwalkers*, Ford Madox Ford's *Parade's End* and Joseph Roth's *Radetsky March*, that psychoanalyse the condition of Europe on the brink of the First World War.

Like his protagonist, Musil came from a military-scientific background. He made his name as a writer in 1906 with *Young Törless*, a short, sharp tale of bullying and buggery at a military academy. Brilliant though it is, nothing in it or the novellas and plays that followed could have led anyone to expect this gigantic novel of ideas.

The title by which it is known in English is problematic, for Ulrich is not without qualities. Intelligent, handsome, athletic, cultured and urbane, he has them in abundance. The German title, *Der Mann ohne Eigenschaften*, is better translated as 'the man without characteristics'. At 32, Ulrich is bored with life. Espousing a scientific, rationalist outlook, he despises 'those who comfort their souls with . . . religious, philosophic and fictitious emotions', because they cannot stomach the hard truth of the intellect. Yet, characteristic of his age, he also betrays an inclination towards mysticism. According to one of the chapter headings, he is 'a man with all the qualities, but they are a matter of indifference to him'. It is precisely this indifference that makes him dangerous.

Ulrich is finally propelled into action by a letter from his father, who discreetly suggests that he will cut off his son's allowance if he doesn't get a job. Against his instincts, Ulrich becomes involved, with the assistance of his high-minded cousin Diotima, in the Collateral Committee set up to plan the jubilee of the Emperor Franz Josef in 1918. The aged emperor has reigned since 1848 – the year of revolutions throughout Europe – but, like Musil and his original readers (the first volume was published in 1930), we know these festivities will never take place: Franz Josef will die in 1916 in the midst of the First World War, and by the end of 1918 his hapless successor Karl will have been dispatched into exile.

As Ulrich steps through the fustian pomp of the Hofburg to be interviewed, it is the old Austria, not the new, that ensnares him. Musil has invented his own name for this mouldering empire: Kakania, derived from the initials K&K (*Kaiserlich und Königlich* – Imperial and Royal), used to denote everything official. It also makes playful reference to *Kaka*, German children's slang for excrement.

Diotima is in fact Ermelinde Tuzzi, the wife of a rising bureaucrat. When Ulrich meets her, she is having an affair with the Prussian financier Paul von Arnheim – as we already know, since Musil slyly affords us a glimpse of the pair enjoying a clandestine tryst in Vienna in the opening pages of the novel. Ulrich and von Arnheim become rivals for both control of the committee and Diotima's affections.

With Part III, the novel – and Ulrich's life – enters a new phase. On the death of his father, he meets his sister Agathe, whom he has not seen for years. Their emotional and intellectual sympathy slowly, inexorably spirals towards forbidden love, and they set up home together. Agathe describes their attachment as 'no longer a love story; it is the very last love story there can be'. (Musil himself was haunted by the knowledge that he had had a sister, who died in infancy before he was born.) While the endless deliberations of the Collateral Committee rumble on, the enduring image of this part of the book is of Ulrich and Agathe in the seemingly eternal stasis of their mystical union, moving their deckchairs around the lawn to follow the light like sunflowers.

There the Wilkins-Kaiser translation breaks off, and what comes next remained a mystery to me for years. It is a curious reading experience. Most novels – even long, leisurely ones such as *The Magic Mountain* – accelerate towards their end. *The Man without Qualities* does the opposite, so that, as the book progresses, time appears to expand and the catastrophe that we, with the benefit of hindsight, know will come, is postponed indefinitely. It is like Zeno's paradox, in which an arrow must travel half the distance, then half the remaining distance, then half that distance again, never reaching its target. 'What the story that makes up this novel amounts to,' Musil wrote in his notebook in 1932, 'is that the story that was supposed to be told in it is not told.'

Musil struggled against the odds to complete the book. Shortly after Part III appeared at the end of 1932, the Nazis came to power in Germany. Musil, whose wife Martha was Jewish, was forced to relocate to Vienna, and his books were banned. In September 1938, after the annexation of Austria, the Musils fled to Switzerland, and he lost most of his readership, his income and many of his notes. That year, he submitted twenty chapters of Part IV to his publisher, but he withdrew them at proof stage. He was still revising them when he died suddenly in April 1942 of a cerebral haemorrhage while performing the morning gymnastics he kept up with fanatical rigour. His wife, who found him, said that he had a look of 'mockery and mild astonishment' on his face.

Musil's widow published the suppressed chapters in 1943. The Wilkins-Kaiser edition tantalizingly promised a further volume, but it never appeared. Then, in 1995, a new translation by Sophie Wilkins and Burton Pike was published. More literal in places than the earlier version, it lacks its lightness of touch but contains the posthumous chapters, along with a mass of sketches. It was a revelation. After the labyrinthine bureaucratic inertia of the second part and the idyllic, mystical interlude of the third, the fourth plunges us back into the world of action, with the increasingly ominous activities of the young proto-fascist Hans Sepp and a deranged plot to spring Moosbrugger from jail. Then, like a great continent, it breaks off into the sheer cliffs, jagged promontories and rocky islets of its unfinished – and sometimes mutually incompatible – fragments.

If there is a challenge in getting through this mighty book, it is not its length, nor its reputed difficulty, but its sheer readability; it is richly comic, and each of its short chapters is so packed with ideas, insights and witticisms that one wants to reread and savour it. On to the great panoramic fiction of the nineteenth century, Musil has grafted the twentieth-century novel of ideas, subjecting an entire civilization to scientific and psychoanalytic examination. To this he adds the modernists' attempts to capture the individual's sensations of the swimming beingness of the moment, as did Proust, Joyce and Woolf. There are no heroes or villains among its rich dramatis personae; all of them, even Moosbrugger, act in a way that makes logical sense from their point of view. Their foibles, pretensions and delusions are laid bare with kindly amusement.

Kundera has described *The Man without Qualities* as 'a matchless existential encyclopaedia about its century; when I feel like rereading this book, I usually open it at random, at any page, without worrying what comes before and what follows'. With each rereading, it becomes more resonant. What we witness in its pages is not so much the demise of a ramshackle empire as the tumultuous birth of the era in which we live. Musil's Kakania is the crucible in which the modern world was forged (think how much modern art, architecture, science, psychology and economic theory came out of Vienna). In his alienation, Ulrich is the precursor of modern man, possessing 'fragments of a new way of thinking, and of feeling'. As Walter observes, 'There are millions of them nowadays. It's the human type that our time has produced.'

C. J. SCHÜLER is the author of three illustrated histories of cartography, and reviews fiction in translation for the *Independent* and other publications: www.cjschuler.com.

Scourge of the Suburbs

ROBIN BLAKE

'Rice Mould' is a story written in 1919 for *Home Magazine*, a periodical aimed at women of the suburban middle class. A party is in progress at the Browns' villa somewhere to the south of London. While the grown-ups get ready to dance to the gramophone in the library, the youngest child, William, a spirited, muddy-kneed, tufty-haired 11-year-old, is trying to smuggle one of Cook's best cream blancmanges in a dirty soap-dish to the girl next door. It does not go well.

The tale so amused *Home Magazine*'s readers that William's creator Richmal Crompton, a young schoolmistress, was asked for another William story, and then another. Three years later she had enough of them to publish a collected edition, *Just William*. It sold so well that she was able, after a debilitating attack of polio, to chuck in her job, settle at Bromley Common and take up writing full-time. In all there would be 39 William books, which have sold over 12 million copies in the UK alone. William has also appeared in nine foreign languages as well as on film, television, stage and radio.

Crompton also wrote 39 novels and 9 story collections not about William, with such titles as *Journeying Wave* and *The Odyssey of Euphemia Tracy*. She cherished them and continued to write them until she was 70 but, redolent as they are of lavender bags and

Thomas Henry

The first three collections of Richmal Crompton's William stories (*Just William*, 1922; *More William*, 1922; and *William Again*, 1923) are available from Macmillan as paperbacks at £5.99 each. Martin Jarvis's readings of the William stories are available on CD from the BBC Radio Collection at £13.25 each.

Boots Lending Library, these titles have not found a niche in the collective memory of readers. William, though, is a different matter. He is lodged in my own memory from long wet summer afternoons spent in his company in Ireland, curled up on a broken-springed sofa in the playroom of my grandparents' house. That association with a holiday is very appropriate because, unlike his fellow 11-year-olds Jennings and Molesworth, William's world is not school-centred. His day-school may on occasion obtrude, but these stories are about free time, and how to fill it without adult interference.

My delight in these stories, and that of huge numbers of my contemporaries, would originally have surprised the author of 'Rice Mould', which she intended for adult readers. The William stories were seized on by children with such pleasure because their central theme – the vast difference between the child's view of reality and the adult's – had never been properly explored in British children's fiction. True, his character has some of the traits of previous fictional 11-year-olds but, apart from boys that pop up in one or two stories by Saki, these were transatlantic models: Tom Sawyer, Huck Finn and, in particular, the lesser known Penrod Schofield of Indianapolis, a character created by the Mid-Western novelist Booth Tarkington. But Tom, Huck and Penrod were as American as root beer, while William's world is nothing if not British.

The familiar boy of William's age, who appeared in stories by the likes of Henty and Ballantyne, was an upright, honourable, conformable lad, as truthful and clean in mind and body as Baden-Powell's ideal scout. He would not dream of questioning any code of behaviour his parents wanted him to follow. Contrast William, grubby, graceless and in tattered garments, who sees himself with steely resolve as – in the titles of some of the books – rebel, outlaw, gangster and (in the very last, 1970 title) lawless.

William differs sharply, too, from the anodyne children in the books of Crompton's equally successful contemporary, Enid Blyton. The typical Blyton story pits a group of plucky but conformist youngsters against the nefarious activities of stereotyped vagrants, gypsies, foreigners and ex-convicts. William on the other hand revels in the company of all forms of marginal low-life. In 'William's Burglar' (which appears in *William Again*, 1923) he frankly tells the felon with the missing ears, whom he spots lurking outside the White Lion pub, 'I like you. I like the way you talk. I like the things you say and I want to know about what you do.'

Once, when asked how the mind of William Brown worked, Crompton explained, 'There is a theory that on our way from the cradle to the grave we pass through all the stages of evolution, and the boy of 11 is at the stage of the savage – loyal to his tribe, ruthless to his foes, governed by mysterious taboos, an enemy of civilization and all its meaningless conventions.'

Crompton's reference is to Recapitulation Theory, summed up by its chief nineteenth-century proponent Ernst Haeckel in the almost impenetrable phrase 'ontogeny recapitulates phylogeny'. Haeckel's idea was adopted by many intellectuals, including Sigmund Freud, and even as late as the 1960s the popular child development expert Dr Benjamin Spock could write 'each child, as he develops, is re-tracing the whole history of mankind'. It's possible Crompton was making fun of what now seems an idea more appropriate to the back of a cereal packet. Yet, as a metaphor for William's distinctiveness, her delineation of 'the stage of the savage' isn't a bad way of sketching her hero's principal traits.

William's family consists of Father (a disciplinarian when he can be bothered), Mother (long-suffering and frequently distraught) and older siblings Robert (constantly lovelorn) and Ethel (pretty but practical). His tribe, on the other hand, are the Outlaws – Ginger, Henry and Douglas, and dog Jumble – who meet under William's rarely challenged leadership at the Old Barn. The Outlaws almost never fall out, and certainly not for long, though they often argue and sometimes fight in exactly the way real boys will tussle.

Their female associates are less consistently seen, but they include

William's girl-next-door Joan, who brings out the knight-errant in him, and various visiting young girls who similarly attract his attention. Where he invariably comes to grief is in his dealings with Violet Elizabeth Bott, a child formidable beyond her years (she's about 6), who exerts a mesmeric control over William and is expert in the deployment of advanced psychological stratagems, not the least of which is the threat that she will 'thcream and thrcream and THRCREAM till I'm thick'.

William often pits himself against a zealous official or an officious relative – anyone deluded enough to think that the boy can be tamed. By chance, cunning, iron nerve and an obstinate refusal to be beaten William usually (but not invariably) defeats these monsters of vanity, sometimes at considerable cost to himself in lost privileges and stopped pocket money. Amongst his own generation, the constant enemy is Hubert Lane and his gang, the Laneites. Hubert is more or less the negative impression of William: prissily dressed, priggish in manner, and fastidious when it comes to muck and puddles. In devising his victories over the Laneites William is never slow to exploit this last weakness in Hubert.

William does not consistently adopt any particular code of behaviour. There are times when he aspires to sainted nobility, others when he yearns to slum it. What he really hates is mediocrity and boredom, and his restless imagination continually seeks fresh stimulation.

He lives in a small community in transition from sleepy rusticity to an expanding London suburb. Along with many other residents William's father travels up by train every weekday to his office, and down again in the evening in time for dinner. At home, all he wants is what he rarely gets – a quiet life. William's mother seems to live to host tea parties and other social functions, while keeping the house, managing the servants and sympathizing with Robert's and Ethel's (usually romantic) woes.

The village is full of retirees such as General Moult and Miss Hathaway, who devote their time to promoting order, personal respectability and modest self-improvement, none of which are at all admired by William. He is also notably unafraid of the suburb's three greatest and most disabling bogeys: property crime, social humiliation and nasty surprises.

Crompton has a beady eye for flaky ideas and theories as they catch fire in small communities, burn fiercely, then peter out. William's suburb is thus visited by the New Era Society (enlightened

Thomas Henry

education), the Society of Ancient Souls (reincarnation), the League of Perfect Love (the sacredness of animal life) and, at the very last in *William the Lawless*, the inchoate and perhaps hippy-inspired Brighter Thought Movement. These vapid attempts to plug the existential gaps in suburban living invariably self-destruct when, either through a well-meaning desire to help or vengeful spoiling tactics, William intervenes.

The William stories as they developed reached a plateau of considerable sophistication in the 1930s and 1940s, and then gradually unravelled in the 1950s and 1960s as the author aged and was also (perhaps) obliged to tailor the books for younger or less competent readers. In these latter stages of William's literary life, it was the very element that had previously been their hallmark – the pitiless exposure of the stupidity, vanity and selfishness of adults in their relations with children – that was eroded. The adults of the later stories are diluted Blyton-like characters and no longer looming figures whom the child's eye magnifies into ogres of injustice and unreason.

What sort of an adult would William himself have made? At one point Richmal Crompton offers this suggestion: 'He disliked facts, and he disliked being tied down to detail, and he disliked answering questions. As a politician, a great future would have lain before him.' This, from 'The May King' in the third collection *William Again*, shows Crompton sacrificing the larger reality of William's character for the sake of a joke – which she would not have done at the peak of her powers. As a matter of fact, I think William might, at least for a while, have made a politician, not for the reasons Crompton gives but because he is a dogged arguer who enjoys nothing more than being the centre of attention and sees himself as fundamentally an idealist and a doer. Fizzing with schemes and eccentricities, and with luck on his side (for some reason, at this point, Boris Johnson springs to mind), he might have had a public career like a firework rocket. He would then, of course, have fallen to earth like one.

There are, as it happens, two prototypes for the grown-up William. One was Crompton's brother Jack, whose adult career would have delighted William, with phases as a mounted policeman in East Africa, traveller across the length and breadth of China, writer of his own adventure novels (as 'John Lambourne'), and finally dedicated expert on insect life. A second and, I think, even better model may be found in a book by Crompton's niece Margaret Disher, *Growing Up with Just William* (1990). Here Disher provides a compelling portrait of her brother Tommy Disher, a boy-man who had a humdrum career in a provincial bank yet was never properly socialized and required 'an adventure a day'. Tommy's misplaced idealism and bald honesty – deeply Williamesque qualities – were legendary: in the case of the latter, as his sister says, 'it was disconcerting to be told [in conversation] "I'm sorry, but I'm not the slightest bit interested in what you're saying".'

Two other talents must be coupled with Crompton's in accounting for William's continuing success: the peerless illustrator Thomas Henry, who illustrated William until his death in 1962 (when the job passed to Henry Ford), and the actor Martin Jarvis, who has done more than any to extend William's lease of life today. The fact must

be faced that the William books are a wordy and slow-moving proposition for a child more used to rapid-fire digital entertainment.
However, the judiciously edited readings of the William stories by
Jarvis for 15-minute radio slots – also available on CD to beguile long
car journeys – cleverly fulfil Richmal Crompton's original intention
to entertain all readers and not just a juvenile audience. For, as these
performances emphasize, William cannot be reduced to a child's
comic cipher, a mere story-book alter-ego. William is a human gad-
fly, a necessary social irritant who, just by being himself, stings and
disrupts complacent authority in all its forms.

ROBIN BLAKE is the author of the Cragg and Fidelis eighteenth-century crime
stories. However, he once had very muddy knees, unruly hair and an intense
longing to be outlawed.

Thomas Henry

Not So Plain Jane

DAISY HAY

Jane Eyre was the novel that opened my eyes to literature. It was the first classic I picked up that I couldn't put down. I read it from cover to cover in one heady weekend when I was 13: I had a nightmare about Grace Poole on Saturday night, and a sulk on Sunday afternoon when my mother made me put it down to talk to some cousins who'd come for tea. By Sunday evening I was done and I knew, with a certainty I still remember vividly, that literature was *my* thing. In the months that followed I devoured *Villette, Shirley, The Professor, Wuthering Heights, Agnes Grey, The Tenant of Wildfell Hall*, the juvenilia – any scraps of Brontë I could get my hands on. I joined the Brontë Society, ploughed my way through each issue of the Brontë Journal, *Transactions*, and made my long-suffering parents take me to the Parsonage at Haworth.

More recently, a few months ago, I was at a dinner at an Oxford college where the subject of life-changing books came up. Over half the literary women present cited *Jane Eyre* as *their* revelatory book. This got me wondering why it has had such an impact on multiple generations of readers and why it inspired quite such obsessive teenage devotion to all things Brontë in me. So I've been rereading it to see if I can locate the source of its extraordinary power.

Trying to do so is, of course, a bit like trying to be funny while writing about comedy: any attempt seems doomed to fail, and has stumped far more eminent commentators than me. From the moment

Charlotte Brontë, *Jane Eyre* (1847)
Everyman · Hb · 284pp · £10.99 · ISBN 9781857150100

of its first publication *Jane Eyre* was a sensation, widely praised by its original critics for its freshness and energy. G. H. Lewes, reviewing the novel in *Fraser's Magazine*, thought it was 'reality – deep, significant reality' that made it so extraordinary. Virginia Woolf – no slouch when it came to literary criticism – wrote that rereading it paralysed her critical faculties. 'We open *Jane Eyre*; and in two pages every doubt is swept clean from our minds . . . Nor is this exhilaration short-lived. It rushes us through the entire volume, without giving us time to think, without letting us lift our eyes from the page.'

Angela Carter testified to the novel's compulsive readability when she wrote that 'of all the great novels in the world, *Jane Eyre* veers the closest towards trash' – a compliment, if ever there was one. Writing in 1997 Heather Glen, one of the most eminent Brontë scholars of her generation, crystallized the novel's unique position in the canon: 'If the readership for many major novelists is now created, through teaching, by the academy,' she argued, '*Jane Eyre*, one suspects . . . would, without any such sponsorship, still be discovered and read.'

It's no accident that three of the four writers I've just quoted are women. It may not be politically correct to say it (and there are many men among Brontë's fans), but there is something about *Jane Eyre* which makes it emphatically a Girl's Book: a novel which is discovered, loved and cherished with a particular intensity by young women, and by the older women they become. That something, I think, is Jane herself: the wronged child who grows up to become one of the most vibrant heroines of English literature.

It is integral to Jane's charm that she doesn't look like a heroine. As a child she is sallow and underfed, in contrast to her beribboned, golden-locked cousins, beside whom she stands as a kind of reproachful ghost. This is certainly how she appears to her cruel Aunt Reed, who is haunted on her death-bed by memories of the child she betrayed. Nor does Jane grow into a beauty. She describes herself as 'plain' and 'puny' and actively resists Mr Rochester's attempts to drape her in jewels and satin, preferring instead to remain in the dull,

Mary Kuper

Quakerish dresses of her governess calling. Only her eyes – so often a useful get-out clause for the literary creators of unbeautiful heroines – give some intimation of her passionate inner life.

Passionate, however, Jane truly is. Early on in the novel the saintly Helen Burns chastises her for thinking 'too much of the love of human beings', for being 'too impulsive, too vehement'. Yet it is Jane's capacity for love which makes her such a vital creation. She may be 'disconnected, poor and plain' but she never allows her emotions to become hedged or confined by circumstance. She knows absolutely that she has a right to love and be loved, even if she berates herself for dreaming of Mr Rochester, so far her social superior. It is significant that when Jane and Rochester finally acknowledge their mutual passion, it is she who claims him, not the other way round. 'Do you think', she cries, 'because I am poor, obscure, plain, and little, I am soulless and heartless? – You think wrong! – I have as much soul as you – and full as much heart!'

Again and again, Jane's story bears out the truth of this. She will not compromise her own integrity by consenting to live as Rochester's mistress, preferring to keep her heart untarnished by immoral passion. And she will not accept the bloodless overtures of her cousin, St John Rivers, who proposes a marriage barren of love and mutual affection. In the end, she triumphs because of her determination to remain true to both her heart and her morals, as she wins Rochester on her own terms.

Jane's passions drive *Jane Eyre*, and point to one reason for its enduring popularity among the generations of young women who have looked to it for an articulation of their own burgeoning emotions. As intriguing, however, is Jane's restlessness, and her cogently expressed anger at the plight of women. It is her desire for freedom and adventure that leads her to abandon her quiet life as a teacher at Lowood School and accept the position of governess at Thornfield, and even when she achieves her 'new servitude' she remains rebellious and unreconciled to her lot:

> Women are supposed to be very calm generally: but women feel just as men feel; they need exercise for their faculties, and a field for their efforts as much as their brothers do, they suffer from too rigid a restraint, too absolute a stagnation, precisely as men would suffer; and it is narrow-minded in their more privileged fellow-creatures to say that they ought to confine themselves to making puddings and knitting stockings, to playing on the piano and embroidering bags.

The force of Jane's argument, here and elsewhere, continues to strike a chord with young readers who, like her, are in the process of working out what they want to do, how they want to live, and who they want to be. Jane never relinquishes her right to make these decisions for herself, even when everyone around her refuses her permission to do so.

But *Jane Eyre* is not simply the tale of one woman's emotional and intellectual awakening, dazzlingly paced and plotted and technically brilliant. It is also a difficult, contradictory novel, which reveals some rather unpleasant truths about human behaviour. The fortune that Jane so conveniently inherits comes from the slave-plantations of Madeira, and the depiction of Bertha Mason, Rochester's mad wife, has made Brontë's critics uneasy from the start. In the twentieth century literary critics grappled with the racial undertones of Bertha's depiction as a wild Creole woman, 'tall, dark and majestic' when Rochester first meets her, but a vicious, grizzled creature by the time

Jane encounters her at Thornfield. Others have noted that Bertha's treatment by Rochester is at best inhumane and at worst lethally negligent of both her safety and her sanity, as he leaves her incarcerated in a cell with only a drunken crone (the nightmare-inducing Grace Poole) for company.

It all raises some tricky questions about Brontë's hero, the Byronic Mr Rochester. He may be swarthy and powerful, but is he really worthy of either of his wives? He attempts to lie and cheat his way into a bigamous marriage with Jane, and has nothing but contempt for Bertha. He toys with the affections of beautiful Blanche Ingram, is dismissive of his ward, 10-year-old Adèle, and is rather too given to fits of violent emotion at moments of crisis. Jane is only permitted to marry him once he has become an emasculated shadow of his former self, maimed and blinded by fire.

Yet for all that there is something irresistible about Rochester, and about the highly charged nature of his relationship with Jane. He might not be an ideal husband and by the end of the story he has been ruthlessly stripped of his most overtly heroic qualities, but Rochester has nevertheless provided a template for the brooding hero familiar to readers of everything from Georgette Heyer to Mills and Boon.

Indeed, one of the things that makes *Jane Eyre* so luxurious to read is that it develops many of the literary types we now take for granted in popular fiction: the plain-spoken heroine, the enigmatic hero, the mad woman in the attic. If, as Angela Carter says, *Jane Eyre* veers delightfully 'towards trash' then that's partly because 'trash' has taken its cue from *Jane Eyre*. (The novel has also, of course, inspired some very fine work, notably Jean Rhys's *Wide Sargasso Sea* and, more recently, Margot Livesey's *The Flight of Gemma Hardy*.) Yet none of Brontë's imitators get close to recreating the magic of her central romance or the power of Jane's adventurous, intelligent voice. Rereading *Jane Eyre* now, that voice still feels contemporary, as does Jane's quest for emotional fulfilment on her own terms.

*

On the Monday morning following my revelatory weekend with *Jane Eyre*, I bounced into school and informed my wise and wonderful English teacher of my discovery. 'That's lovely, dear,' she replied. 'But by the time you're 21 you'll realize that Jane Austen is even better.' She was quite right. *Jane Eyre* was the book I grew up with and, in the end, grew out of. Returning to it now has been overwhelmingly pleasurable, partly because it is truly a great novel, and partly because it has made me remember my old devotion to it. It may not be the most polished novel in the English canon, and Brontë may not write with the subtlety of Austen or Woolf. But *Jane Eyre* was the novel that unlocked great literature for me. It held the promise of all the literature waiting to be discovered: literature which would move and inspire me in ways that, at 13, I couldn't predict.

And at a guess, I'd say that this is why it was also such a crucial book for those literary women at High Table in Oxford, and for the generations of readers who have loved it from childhood. It opens a door on to a world of new experiences, a world where books fire your imagination, your intellect and your heart. Once you've stepped over the threshold of that world, you never look back.

DAISY HAY is a lecturer in English Literature at the University of Exeter and the author of *Young Romantics*. Sadly, her membership of the Brontë Society has now lapsed.

Feeling a Little Wembley

OLIVER PRITCHETT

In the 1960s, at a time when I took myself more seriously, I went to work for the *Observer* in what I mistakenly believed was a rather important position. One afternoon, soon after my arrival, a stranger walked into the office I shared with two other people. He was neat, quite short and stocky, and, I seem to remember, he wore a pale tweed jacket. He had a pleasant light tenor voice and the air, perhaps, of a popular geography master at a prep school.

The stranger strolled nonchalantly round the small room dictating letters to the person I regarded as 'my' secretary. 'Dear Mrs Coleridge, Thank you for your letter. I must confess I have never met a man who earned his living as a flange wrangler, but it sounds a most interesting job . . . Dear Mr Clifton, It was so kind of you to send me your father's copy of the Swahili phrase-book, which I shall always treasure . . . Dear G. W. Hurst, I very much enjoyed your observations about Japanese waltzing mice . . .'

This man, I soon discovered, was Paul Jennings, creator of the 'Oddly Enough' column, up in town from his home in East Bergholt and replying to his fan mail. (This could be irritating for any self-important young journalist to listen to, particularly for one with no fans of his own.) The performance was repeated every two or three weeks; he would arrive, dictate a few politely surreal letters, click his briefcase shut, give a jovial wave and leave.

Paul Jennings, *Oddly Enough* (1950), *Even Oddlier* (1952), *Oddly Bodlikins* (1953), *Next to Oddliness* (1955), *I Said Oddly, Diddle I?* (1961), *The Jenguin Pennings* (1963) and *Golden Oddlies* (1983) are all out of print.

Of course, I made up those letters, but they reflect the flavour of 'Oddly Enough' and, in fact, on two or three occasions over the years he did write about the phenomenon of Japanese waltzing mice. The humour of his column, which appeared in the *Observer* from 1949 until 1966, was based on whimsy and wordplay. Whimsy has come to be despised by smart modern humorists, but in Jennings it came fortified with a sharp intelligence and a rich imagination.

A few years later, I found myself employed in the whimsy trade and I came to appreciate the quiet brilliance of Paul Jennings. I wished I had taken the opportunity to get to know him better.

The great J. B. Morton wrote the Introduction to the first book of collected 'Oddly Enough' pieces (and articles for other publications, including *Punch*) which appeared in 1950. He observed that the humour of Paul Jennings was English, which was certainly true, and he added: 'Mr Jennings has Chesterton's habit of seeing familiar things as though he had suddenly noticed them for the first time, so they are a surprise to him.' This neatly sums up the Jennings approach and he must have been thrilled at such praise from the creator of the 'Beachcomber' column where everything was dazzlingly surprising.

The sport of wordplay can be seen in the titles of Jennings' books – such as *Even Oddlier, Oddly Bodlikins, Next to Oddliness* and *I Said Oddly, Diddle I?* In 1963 Penguin published a pretty definitive selection called *The Jenguin Pennings* and in 1983 Methuen brought out a retrospective volume entitled *Golden Oddlies*.

His most often quoted conceit was his piece called 'Ware, Wye and Watford' in which he explored 'the vast English treasury of sub-conscious meaning' in place names. If someone tells you 'I'm feeling a little wembley today', you know you are dealing with a fan of Jennings, who defined the word as 'suffering from a vague malaise'. According to Jennings, beccles is an ailment in sheep, ilkley means having large eyebrows, cromer is a mistake or bungle – as in 'you made a cromer there' - and stevenage is an ancient nominal rental paid to a lord of the manor.

Humorous writers today would scorn the idea of making jokes about the perils of touch typing and the way the words come out skew-whiff but Jennings could pull it off with one neat observation. Qwertyuiop, he suggested, would be a good onomatopoeic word for a corkscrew, the qw-erty suggesting the squeak of the cork being turned in the bottle and the ui-OP being the sound of it coming out.

He loved language and languages. Instructions in German and French on how to use a public telephone enchanted him. After seeing the 1951 film *Quo Vadis* (Hollywood's version of ancient Rome) he was inspired to write his own film treatment, with all the great cinema clichés in Latin.

Daniel Macklin

Nonne aliquis tibi dixit te pulchram esse? the hero says when he first meets the heroine ('Did anyone ever tell you you're beautiful?'). After this we get all the old Hollywood favourites – from 'So that's your game' (*Sic illud est ludus tuus*) to 'You stay out of this, sister' (*Tu mane ex hoc, soror*).

Paul Jennings was born in 1918 and educated at King Henry VIII School, Coventry, and at the Benedictine school Douai Abbey. He first contributed to *Punch* when he was a lieutenant in the Royal Signals. He worked for a time for the Central Office of Information and it was probably there that he became a connoisseur of official jargon. After a spell in advertising he joined the *Observer* in 1949.

One of his early pieces, which appeared in the *Spectator* in 1948, was more satire than whimsy. It was called 'Resistentialism' and was a blistering spoof on the currently fashionable Existentialism. Developed by Paul-Marie Ventre, who haunted the Café aux Fines Herbes on the Left Bank in Paris, Resistentialism was based on the proposition *Les choses sont contre nous* or 'Things are against us'.

Some people who have seen Ventre's plays, Jennings wrote, are apt to think that Resistentialism is largely a matter of sitting inside a wet sack and moaning, but of course it is much more than that. Its influence has also spread to art and music.

He goes on to describe, in the most elaborately scholarly terms, the essence of the philosophy, how it involves such concepts as the unfoldability of newspapers and how toast tends to fall marmalade-side down more often on more expensive carpets. In short, it is an early exposition of Sod's Law in intellectual fancy dress.

I can't imagine Paul Jennings ever walking briskly down the street; he was a natural stroller, always on the lookout for interesting names on brass plates on buildings, and if he spotted one of those mysterious cast-iron notices you still see rusting on bridges or railway crossings he would pause and patiently read it to the end. A sign saying 'Activated Sludge' caught his attention and unleashed a fantasy, as did the 'Submerged Log Company' and 'Glass Benders'.

He loved lists, particularly those found in obscure Board of Trade pamphlets. How happy he would be today, with the minutiae of European Union directives and treaties. He relished joke-shop catalogues, listing 'dehydrated worms, impossible spoon joke, wobbly matchbox with key, best joke moustaches . . .' He delighted in the list of thirty-seven Shetland telephone exchanges before they became part of the Aberdeen zone in July 1951 – 'Mid Yell, Vidlin, Voe, Fetlar . . .' and he was cleared for take-off on another flight of fancy.

I am intrigued by Jennings's friend Harblow who appears on several occasions in his pieces, usually as 'my friend Harblow'. Like clubby chaps of the past, he is referred to only by his surname. I imagine a tweedy fellow of few words, with a pipe and a moustache. An old-fashioned man's man. Was he made up or did he really exist? Clues in the columns suggest he was a friend from army days and in early writings there are several accounts of motoring in France with Harblow in Jennings's 1928 Austin Seven.

It's possible, from a study of the various Oddlies, to piece together a partial portrait of a subtly comic character: Harblow had a mongrel dog called Jim, was a bit of a hypochondriac, a noisy gargler, thought he knew about plumbing but didn't. He also knew his rights. In a piece called 'Money Back', Jennings describes a visit to a London tearoom with Harblow where they encounter an unsatisfactory peach melba. He steels himself as he realizes that his friend is about to lodge a complaint. 'Harblow, I thought bitterly, is the sort of man who would ask for his money back at the cinema if the projectionist, the manager and all the usherettes were shot dead by bandits two minutes before the end of the film.'

Paul Jennings also liked to turn to light verse and he was capable of coming up with some lines which would certainly have impressed that supreme rhymester Ogden Nash. Expressing his indignation at his discovery that it was possible to buy tinned beetroot, he wrote of:

Foods which depress you, like the books of Schopenhauer,
And are not worth your trouble with the tin and the openhauer.

And I share his admiration for postmen:

Postmen don't seem to mind cold and rain, they seem
    impervious.
They are the nicest people in the Civil Servious.

I saw Paul Jennings just once after we had both left the *Observer*. It was in a South London pub, close to Trinity Church, in Southwark, and he was one of a jolly crowd. I realized they must have been a choir who had just finished rehearsing in the nearby church. He was laughing and joking with his friends. Music made him happy. I wanted to go up to him and tell him how much I had come to admire his work, but I was too shy. So I'm saying it now.

OLIVER PRITCHETT has given up full-time whimsy production in order to concentrate on idle fancy.

A Friendship of Opposites

GRANT MCINTYRE

Never one for naval yarns I didn't at first spot Patrick O'Brian's Aubrey/Maturin novels, which are set in the wars at sea against Napoleon and then the United States. But once I'd tried one I bought them by the handful. It was like that for most of his readers. O'Brian was not successful at first; critics took him for a kind of retread C. S. Forester, and in fact his books did look a bit dated, published next to *Radical Chic & Mau-Mauing the Flak Catchers* for instance, or *One Hundred Years of Solitude*. A surprising few – Iris Murdoch, Charlton Heston, William Waldegrave and David Mamet, for example – were passionate about them from the start, but ten years passed before most of us realized something new and extraordinary had appeared. Now hardly anyone brackets him with Forester; rather, some compare him to Jane Austen for subtle and comic prose, or Tolstoy for the way he makes past speak to present. His sales have passed 4 million, in twenty languages or more, there's been a film, and a whole sub-section of scholarship has bloomed, including a

---

Patrick O'Brian's Aubrey/Maturin novels comprise: *Master and Commander* (1969); *Post Captain* (1972); *HMS Surprise* (1973); *The Mauritius Command* (1977); *Desolation Island* (1978); *The Fortune of War* (1979); *The Surgeon's Mate* (1980); *The Ionian Mission* (1981); *Treason's Harbour* (1983); *The Far Side of the World* (1984); *The Reverse of the Medal* (1986); *The Letter of Marque* (1988); *The Thirteen-Gun Salute* (1989); *The Nutmeg of Consolation* (1991); *Clarissa Oakes* (1992); *The Wine-Dark Sea* (1993); *The Commodore* (1994); *The Yellow Admiral* (1996); *The Hundred Days* (1998); *Blue at the Mizzen* (1999); and *The Final Unfinished Voyage of Jack Aubrey* (2004). All are available as paperbacks from HarperCollins.

dictionary, a gazetteer, a cookery book, a critical bibliography, a recreation of Aubrey's favourite frigate and a biographical skirmish or two.

At the beginning of the first novel, *Master and Commander* (1969), an overweight naval lieutenant, Jack Aubrey, is at a private concert next to 'an ill-looking son-of-a-bitch' who turns out to be Stephen Maturin, an Irish-Catalan doctor, prickly and brilliant. Jack takes badly Stephen's demand that he stop beating time and for all love STOP GOING POM-POM-POM! But before the inevitable duel he gets glorious news that he's been appointed to his first command; suddenly he's happy to apologize, lays on lunch, discovers that Stephen is for the moment on his uppers, and persuades him to join his new ship as surgeon. 'Certainly,' says Stephen, 'for a student of human nature, what could be better? The subjects of his inquiry shut up together, unable to escape his gaze, their passions heightened by the dangers of war . . . their isolation from women, and their curious but uniform diet. And by the glow of patriotic fervour, no doubt' – with a nod to Jack. So the diminutive sloop *Sophie* acquires a doctor, scientist and – as it turns out – undercover agent, far above her station.

Their friendship survives war, disaster and rivalry in love, problems with politics and snoring, 'very grave differences in domestic behaviour' – and continues to the last line O'Brian wrote, in his twenty-first, unfinished book. It's a friendship of opposites. Jack is worse than fallible ashore, but at sea he's a phenomenon, a natural leader whose men will follow him anywhere. He's decisive, open, forceful, and runs a crack ship without flogging, since 'a happy ship is your only hard-fighting ship'. He's no blue-light, psalm-singing, tract-and-cocoa captain (as, interestingly, Jane Austen's brothers were); to him just to *be* on an enemy deck, sword in hand, brings a wild and savage joy. Above all he has the miraculous quality of luck, 'not . . . commonplace good fortune, far from it, but a different concept altogether, one of an almost religious nature, like the favour of some god or even in some cases like possession; and if it [comes] in too hearty it might prove fatal – too fiery an embrace entirely'.

Stephen, on the other hand, is a secretive savant with pale reptilian eyes and a tea-cosy wig, addicted to opium and coca. Unlike Jack he's very effective on land, but aboard ship he is always falling down hatchways or into the sea. When the men discover his lifesaving skill at surgery, they look on him as a kind of shaman. Even Jack says having him aboard is like sailing with a piece of the True Cross. 'I seen him whip a man's skull off,' says Able Seaman Plaice, 'rouse out his brains, set 'em to rights, stow 'em back again, clap on a silver plate, and sew on his scalp, which it was drooling over one ear, obscuring his dial, with a flat-seam needle and a pegging awl . . . I seen him sew on a man's arm when it was hanging by a thread, passing remarks in Greek.'

Different as they are in every way, each sees in the other a man who will venture anything for what he knows is right; both are men of integrity, humane where possible but ruthless where not, clear-sighted about the world's hazards and their own weaknesses. Each can enhance life for the other: Stephen is not just a doctor, he's a natural philosopher on terms with half Europe's Enlightenment, and his travels with Jack bring him to flora and fauna he would never otherwise see (or dissect).

Meanwhile, as captain, Jack is enveloped with a deference 'different in kind from that accorded to a fellow human being' which surrounds him 'like a glass bell'. As his particular friend Stephen can make this isolation bearable, especially as both are musicians, Jack on his violin, Stephen on his cello – battered instruments patched by the ship's carpenter and bowed if need be with strands from the longer pigtails aboard. On the other hand Jack is a Tory and Stephen a radical through and through, against authority even at sea – 'Do away with subordination and you do away with tyranny: without subordination we should have no Neros, no Tamerlanes, no Buonapartes.'

'Stuff,' says Jack. 'Subordination is the natural order: there is subordination in Heaven . . . and so it is in the Navy. You have come to the wrong shop for anarchy, brother.'

Of course, the friendship serves a purpose in the novels' structure too. Fiction is full of wonderful duos – Don Quixote and Sancho Panza, Holmes and Watson, Tintin and Haddock – which give bearings on events from two sensibilities. It's the same with Jack and Stephen, and there are other advantages besides. Because neither understands the other's world, we get the benefit of their explanations (not that it really matters if we don't know a shroud from a sheet, and can't guess why a simple thing like a cunt-splice wouldn't take a man-o'-war's bosun long). More important, as Stephen's work as spy and political agent comes to dominate the action, O'Brian can transport him, and us, in Jack's favourite ship the *Surprise* to confront a range of hazards at the ends of the earth, when otherwise they'd be blockading France year in year out, in foul weather or fair, with the rest of the Navy.

Eighteenth-century life at sea was extreme in almost every way, still more so aboard a ship as small as the *Surprise*. She is a captured French frigate, old but fast; only 130 feet long though she carries around 250 men, with a few boys and maybe the gunner's wife to look after them, plus sometimes a hen or two and a goat. Jack's cabin has space and light, but below decks is dark, crowded and smelly.

Friction is always a risk between so many 'incompatible tempers mewed up together in a box', sometimes for years, but for officers goodwill is helped on by dinners, in full dress whatever the temperature, with plenty of claret and port to drink and maybe soused hog's face or drowned baby to eat (or after months at sea more likely albatross soup or sea-elephant fritters). Above deck there's a different world: the *Surprise* carries an acre of sail and thirty miles of rope, and has a wonderfully beautiful rig, especially on a fine calm day 'with the sun shining through and across all its curves, convexities and infinite variety of brilliantly lit or delicately shadowed white'. Below decks may be airless and fetid, but from the mastheads lookouts can survey 700 square miles of open sea.

A complex wooden world like this needed skilful handling. It had to cope with war, of course, but also with weather. Of the two, weather was likelier to send a ship to the bottom. There might be no wind, so she'd drift on an oily, heaving sea, 'figurehead simpering all round the compass and . . . nearly rolling her masts by the board'. Or there might be far too much wind, as in the scene here. Stephen has appeared on deck, unprepared for the terror about to confront him.

> Under the low grey tearing sky, half driving rain, half driving spray, the whole sea was white – a vast creaming spread as far as the eye could see . . . For a moment the whole could have been a wild landscape, mountainous yet strangely regular; but then he saw that the whole was in motion, a vast majestic motion whose size concealed its terrifying dreamlike speed.

The crew struggle to hold the ship straight before the wind so she won't broach to and capsize. Stephen looks towards the stern and sees

> a grey-green wall towering above the taffrail, racing towards them – swift inevitability. He strained his head back to see its top, curving beyond the vertical as it came yet still balancing with the speed of its approach, a beard of wind-torn spray flying out before it.

O'Brian was a master narrator of action: storms, battle, or both together. I've never felt so personally present as when reading the passage where Jack is pursued in the South Seas by a faster, heavier gunned Dutchman, the *Waakzaamheid*. This time too they are running before a gale, chased by vast waves a quarter of a mile apart and taller than the ships themselves – waves with a reach of a thousand miles or more. When finally the Dutchman's bow is just yards from Jack's stern, the two captains staring at each other over mountainous peaks of green water, the gunners aim single shots on the rise and fall, knowing that one lucky hit could split a sail or carry away a mast, leaving the enemy helpless in a frantic sea.

Of course that sort of battle was not the norm: far commoner were point-blank broadsides, big guns roaring away, recoiling and jumping, six-foot splinters scything across decks in the smoke, spars crashing, constant shouting. The screaming wounded would be carried below to Stephen, cutting and sawing and stitching in his surgery far below the waterline, his loblolly boy collecting limbs and guts to put over the side after the fight. Broadsides would be followed by boarding – Jack savagely joyful on that enemy deck, invariably flanked by his huge coxswain Barrett Bonden, once a prize-fighter, and by Awkward Davies, another giant, a man of 'dark subhuman rage' with a line of foam at his lips, hacking at living and dead alike. Jack would have his luck. He would need it to take the prizes that temporarily enriched him and still more briefly his men, and he would need it even to survive, with catastrophe and death always inches away.

Stephen's life is not much less eventful than Jack's. He could make himself rich by running a medical practice in London or Dublin or even Barcelona, but he prefers to travel the world for the sake of science. And doing that gives him cover for intelligence work he prefers to do without pay, driven by hatred of Napoleon and an obsession with Catalan independence. He's no foot-soldier either; he has made himself one of the Admiralty's chief assets – worth a ship of the line to us any day of the week, says the First Lord. That's because he's not just a spy but a dab hand at political advice, the ideal man to forestall a coup or nobble a dubious neutral.

Naturally Jack grows aware of his work, though they don't talk about it, and to start with is rather in awe. He 'had supposed he knew him through and through in the old uncomplicated times, and he loved all he knew; but now there were new depths, an underlying hard ruthlessness, an unexpected Maturin; and Jack was quite out of his depth'. The greater Maturin's success, though, the more he's a target, and the more he needs his friend's help.

Let's leave the two of them for now, not in danger but in a fine passage of O'Brian's descriptive writing. Stephen is remembering moments of calm on the little sloop, near the start of their friendship,

> in the warm, deepening twilight, watching the sea; it had barely a ruffle on its surface, and yet the *Sophie* picked up enough moving air with her topgallants to draw a long straight whispering furrow across the water, a line brilliant with unearthly phosphorescence, visible for quarter of a mile behind her. Days and nights of unbelievable purity. Nights when the steady Ionian breeze rounded the square mainsail – not a brace to be touched, watch relieving watch – and he and Jack on deck, sawing away, sawing away, lost in their music, until the falling dew untuned their strings. And the days when the perfection of dawn was so great, the emptiness so entire, that men were almost afraid to speak.

Two further articles on the Aubrey/Maturin novels will follow in Issues 42 and 44.

GRANT MCINTYRE, who is now a sculptor, finds he can read far more widely than he could when he was a publisher.

Dear Jansson San

LINDA LEATHERBARROW

In the 1960s, long before J. K. Rowling showed the world how literary fame might be managed, Tove Jansson, pursued by her own creations the Moomins – white hippopotamus-shaped trolls with tails but no mouths – thought there was only one solution: to buy her own island with the proceeds and escape, if not permanently, at least for several months at a time. Who needed a postman when this was the kind of letter he brought?

> We look forward to your valuable reply soonest concerning Moomin motifs on toilet paper in pastel shades.

© Jansson family archive

Tove Jansson, who was born in 1914 in Helsinki and studied art in Stockholm and Paris, wrote her first Moomin book during the Second World War, when Finland was at war with the Soviet Union. Children loved the Moomins, who survive even the most drastic upheavals by always being good-humoured and tolerant, and by 1954 Jansson was drawing a Moomin comic strip for adults in an English newspaper, the *Evening News* (circulation 12 million). Soon her cartoon had spread to 40 other countries and 120 further publications. Now,

Tove Jansson, *A Winter Book: Selected Stories* (2006) ·
Trans. Silvester Mazzarella, David McDuff & Kingsley Hart
Sort of Books · Pb · 192pp · £8.99 · ISBN 9780954899523

like J. K. Rowling, she wanted to write fiction for adults, but she was being asked to design Moomin paper dolls and wallpaper, and there was no end to the letters and requests from Moomin fans.

> Couldn't we meet and chat about the old days at school? I'm Margit, the one who punched you in the stomach in the playground.

To Jansson's relief, her youngest brother, Lars – also a gifted artist and writer – took over the cartoon and, in 1958, they founded their company, later converted into the joint-stock company Moomin Characters Ltd. Moomin novels were soon followed by picture books, a song book, several children's plays and even a ballet performed at the Finnish National Opera, for which Jansson designed the stage sets and costumes. And, of course, all this meant more and more fan mail, by the sackful. Amazingly, it was Jansson's practice to reply to each fan letter by hand, even though there were also sackfuls of business correspondence concerning Moomin neckties, candles, wrapping paper, porcelain plates and mugs. Moomins were not just good business, they had become a global brand.

> We are fully aware that you had planned a black troll for our Moomin liquorice advertisement but for technical reasons . . .

Her private island might not have been everybody's first choice – Klovharu, a tiny lump of rock in the storm-lashed Gulf of Finland. Atoll-shaped, it surrounds a deep lake that, in good weather, is ideal for swimming, in bad weather turns into a raging torrent. For twenty-eight years Jansson lived there every summer, her only companion the graphic artist Tuulikki Pietilä, known to the family as Tooti and the inspiration for Too-Ticky, the creative but responsible Moomin. On the island, they painted and drew together, read and wrote, only returning to their separate studios in Helsinki for the winter.

> My cat died! Write at once.

Klovharu is so small they could walk round it in ten minutes. There was only one tree, a rowan, but wild pansies, chives and dog roses grew among the rocks. Their plain wooden cabin had neither running water nor electricity. They used rainwater for their coffee and driftwood for their fires and, if they needed an excursion, they went fishing. Here, at last, Jansson was able to devote herself to writing fiction for adults: four novels and six collections of short stories.

A Winter Book contains a selection of twenty of her best stories. Written between 1968 and 1998, and translated into English by three translators, this is a curious hotch-potch that somehow works, containing semi-autobiographical stories about the secrets of childhood and the obsessions of old age, stories set on land or sea, set in winter or summer. They come together because Jansson understands exactly which small events are worth writing about and how to turn them into art. Her stories are always delightfully unpredictable and, as Ali Smith explains in her excellent introduction, often 'much less melancholy than the average Moomin tale'.

© Per Olav Jansson

They are also full of risk and danger. Bring on the sunken boats and icebergs and obliterating sea fogs. Bring on the snow and ferocious storms – Force 9 on the Beaufort scale. Bring on the surprises that accompany them: a crate of Spanish oranges, a silver carpet of two-gallon canisters full of brandy, a mysteriously stranded squirrel which, in one especially powerful story, becomes a solitary islander's nemesis, eventually making off at night with her boat. Jansson writes with unnerving clarity about intense yet straightforward relationships, the sort that many of us might envy. Her characters, whether young or old, are often stubbornly heroic, never truly bad, only a little excited perhaps, or lonely.

In 'Messages', she gathers together a selection of apparently random snippets culled from letters that may or may not be real. They suggest some of the demands a famous writer might be expected to cope with.

Hi! We're three girls in a mad rush with our essays about you could you help us by saying in just a few words how you started writing and why and what life means to you and then a message to young people you know the kind of thing. Thanks in advance.

It's possible, of course, that it wasn't just fame that Jansson needed to get away from. There was another island, the Family Island, just visible across the water, on which the rest of the Jansson family encamped every summer. Tove and Lars were not the only artists in the family and not the only ones to work from home. Her other brother, Per Olav Jansson, was a photographer; her mother, Signe Hammarsten, a designer and illustrator and possibly the inspiration for the wise and gentle Moominmamma whose handbag always contains exactly what is needed for any emergency or adventure. Jansson's father, Victor Jansson – Moominpappa? – was a well-known sculptor, a spontaneous party-giver, a man who loved sailing through the wildest thunderstorms and who was bohemian enough to keep a monkey in his studio – in other words, an Artist with a capital A.

According to her niece Sophia Jansson, who is the present creative director and chairman of the family Moomin business, Tove Jansson was also an artist with a capital A, one who needed space as well as support. And meanwhile the Moomin spin-offs just went spinning off and off – radio plays and four different television series, including a German/Polish co-production featuring puppets and a Japanese animated version. In Japan you could buy Moomin lunch boxes and chopsticks.

Klovharu provided a much-needed sanctuary, and *A Winter Book* includes some striking photographs of the island taken by her brother, Per Olav, showing the little wooden cabin, the lichen-covered rocks, the pool. There are also portraits from the family archive of an infant Tove with Signe, both of them carefully posed and serenely confident, especially Tove, despite sporting a pudding-bowl haircut and a tidy blouse with smocking. There is one of Tove with the eponymous squirrel, another of her smiling and smoking a cigarette while buttoning herself into a heavy-duty overcoat. A plaster-splattered Victor works in his studio, plays his guitar, or kisses Poppolino (his monkey), or wears a rakish felt hat while rowing with Signe across the open sea in a tiny wooden boat. Tooti appears flying a kite, but muffled up in bobble hat and jacket and seen from the back. This may be because her relationship with Tove was a private affair or simply because, even in summer, it was freezing cold in the Gulf of Finland.

Jansson lived on the island until 1991 by which time she was 77. Perhaps, even for her, a régime without a telephone and only cold outdoor dips was beginning to seem a little harsh.

'Taking Leave', the final story in the collection, is about two elderly women saying goodbye to their island. The narrator becomes afraid of the sea, its waves appear threatening and no longer promise adventure, and then, unforgivably, that fear comes to feel like a betrayal, and an unspoken decision is made. Fishing nets are taken in, carefully hoarded possessions given away, other items labelled and explained for the use of future occupants. 'Don't close the damper; it rusts and sticks', 'The key is by the doorpost', and 'Woollen stockings and socks under the boot rack'. The conclusion is far from miserable. I won't give it away because, taken out of context, it could seem trite, and Jansson's prose is never trite, always wise – and light and cool as the wind.

She died in Helsinki in 2001 aged 86. Today, there is a Moomin museum in Tampere and two Moomin theme parks – one in Finland, the other in Japan where her Moomins have acquired not only mouths, but also American accents. I don't suppose Jansson ever imagined that her peaceful island refuge might one day become a destination for literary tourists and fans, but it has, and they do indeed sail across to visit it. There they can see the rusty key to her wooden house still hanging on a piece of driftwood, everything exactly as she left it.

Dear Jansson san
I have collected money for a long time. I will come and sit at your feet to understand. Please when can I come there?

LINDA LEATHERBARROW has an island too, not her own she hastens to add, but it might as well be; few people go there. It sits in the mouth of a bay and can be reached at low tide by following the hoof-prints of deer across the mud.

Building Blocks

GUS ALEXANDER

The idea of telling a story based on a construction project has been with us since the Book of Genesis, but the method chosen to tell the tale imparted in *The Honeywood File*, and its sequel *The Honeywood Settlement*, is by far the most effective and entertaining way I know of describing a process that is at once collaborative and confrontational. Written by H. B. Cresswell, himself a practising architect, *The Honeywood File* and its successor began life as a series of weekly articles that appeared in the *Architects' Journal* between 1925 and 1927, whence they soon gathered enough of a following to be collected and published as books in 1929 and 1930.

The story concerns the building of a ten-bedroomed country house, Honeywood Grange, for a peppery but fair-minded middle-aged financier, Sir Leslie Brash, his neurotic wife Maud and their daughter Phyllis, a bright young thing. The file in question is the architect's 'job file' as it accumulates correspondence in the office of 29-year-old architect James Spinlove, recently established in practice and whose first significant project this is. The job might generate a fee of perhaps £100,000 today.

Most practising architects find themselves with an irate client and/or disgruntled builder at some point, and will be familiar with the dispiriting task of poring over ancient correspondence, trying to unravel the obligations the various parties have to each other in an attempt to stop an argument turning into a lawsuit. When I began

H. B. Cresswell, *The Honeywood File* (1929) and *The Honeywood Settlement* (1931), are both out of print.

working as a trainee architect, I remember waiting in trepidation as my boss looked over a draft of one of my early letters. 'This is much too chatty,' he said, crossing out half my effort with a red Pentel. 'One day we'll find some clever-dick lawyer reading this out in court and tearing us to shreds with it.'

The reader needs no specialist knowledge in order to enjoy *The Honeywood File*. I first read it before sitting my professional exams in 1976 and have dipped into it at five-year intervals ever since – 'just to remind myself what fun it was' – only to find myself going back to the beginning and starting again from scratch. The correspondence appears in chronological order and, apart from a running commentary in the form of footnotes added by the author drawing attention to the correspondent's style or to some hidden agenda, there is no narrative at all.

The cast of characters includes Spinlove, Sir Leslie, John Grigblay of Messrs J. Grigblay & Sons, a builder with whom any architect would be privileged to work, Nibnose & Rasper, the sort of builders I have spent a lifetime trying to avoid, and Bloggs, Grigblay's foreman – the man actually responsible for building Honeywood Grange to Spinlove's design, whose virtually illiterate scrawl one can imagine being composed with a screwed-up face and much licking of a rectangular carpenter's pencil. There are any number of other con-

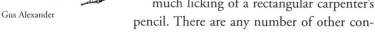

Gus Alexander

tributors – brick merchants trying to pass off seconds as facings, oleaginous suppliers of sewerage equipment whose lavender-scented writing-paper offers components for septic tanks that are much more sophisticated and expensive than they need be, a firm of grand so-licitors, a pompous KC, opportunistic neighbours with their hands out – each with a style of address that reflects his particular interest in the project.

Throughout the construction stage we feel the misanthropic hand of Mr Potch, the local Building Inspector, who moonlights as an unofficial 'architect' in his spare time. Potch and his cronies in the local Rotary Club resent whippersnappers like Spinlove coming down from 'Lunnen' and queering their pitch. Potch's sole purpose in life seems to be to frustrate Spinlove's endeavours wherever possible. Their correspondence reveals the world of cosy provincial back-scratchers and price-fixers whose only interest in the construction industry is to make as much money out of it as possible, whereas Brash, Spinlove and Grigblay are co-operating on a project with a more serious cultural intent than they would probably admit.

Nothing much seems to have changed in the industry since 1930 although, sadly, firms like Grigblay & Sons are far thinner on the ground, and clients like Sir Leslie Brash, if they are not buying luxury executive dwellings with three-car garages, are refurbishing Georgian rectories rather than building new estates. And, of course, nobody writes letters any more.

What *The Honeywood File* does extremely well is to establish the roles and obligations of the principal players in any serious building project. Spinlove must ensure that Brash procures the house that he, Spinlove, has been commissioned to design, but he must also ensure that Grigblay is properly paid for work that he has been asked to do, even though some of it, much to Spinlove's discomfort, may not have been included in the tender documents. At the same time, Grigblay needs to maintain his reputation as an excellent builder and to be careful not to drop the inexperienced Spinlove in it or allow him to be bullied by Brash, who is, of course, paying for everything.

Like *Godfather 2*, *The Honeywood Settlement* is perhaps even more enjoyable than its predecessor. The settlement of a building project's 'final account' takes place during the six-month period after the clients move in and before the final inspection, which occurs only once all outstanding defects have been made good. At this point all final payments are authorized. My own particular interest in this ritual has been the payment of the balance of the architect's fee. It ain't over till it's over.

The main thrust of the book deals with the catastrophe that follows as a result of the application everywhere, at a crucial stage of the construction process, of 'Riddoppo', a new super-paint that Sir Leslie has been flattered into promoting by one of his business cronies, in preference to the tried and tested paint specified by Spinlove, the properties of which are well understood. Despite the most forcefully presented arguments against adopting this course of action, Sir Leslie has to demonstrate who's boss. Perhaps a section of the builder Grigblay's letter to Spinlove, written once the super-paint has begun to demonstrate all the failings he anticipated, will give a flavour of the whole enterprise.

Grigblay to Spinlove (12.3.26)
The matter I am taking the liberty to write to you privately about is this New Novelty Super Paint the old gentleman insisted I use and which is going to be a bit more of a novelty than he bargained for. The ripple is much more than it was, and is forming in ridges. Sir Leslie may think it looks pretty so, but he will change his mind when it begins to fold over on itself and break away in flakes – which is what comes next, for I found a place behind a radiator in the bathroom where it is doing a bit of private rehearsal. The worst place is on the wall of the kitchen where the furnace flue goes up behind. The maids have brushed it over and washed it down till there isn't any paint left, scarcely.

As you know, sir, I refused to take responsibility for Riddoppo and gave warning before the painters left the job that it would all have to come off again – except what came off of itself – and I hope you will bear it in mind, because when Riddoppo gets a move on and shows how super it knows how to be (and we shan't be long now), the dogs will begin to bark;

and as I don't want to be bit, and you, I take it, don't want to either . . . I take the liberty, with all respect to your superior judgement, of dropping you a friendly hint – which is just to take no kind of notice; and if the old gentleman says anything or makes any complaint, to hold out that the paint is no concern of yours any more than it is mine . . . Please be very careful, sir, what letters you write to Sir Leslie; and do not write Any if avoidable, for lawyers are wonderful fellows at proving words mean the opposite of what they do.

I hope no harm done by me addressing you, but thought best, as I am afraid there is trouble ahead.

I am, sir

Yours faithfully

There is also an enclosure from Grigblay to Riddoppo dated 27.2.26.

Gentlemen

We painted out Honeywood with your Riddoppo Super because we were so ordered, and if you want to know what it looks like better go and see as we only carried out architects orders and it is no more business of ours and we will have no more to do with it.

When I first read this saga it was as an architect of about the same age as Spinlove, and I knew little about builders. Thirty years later I know a great deal about them, and I have come to realize not only what a difficult job they do, but also that the good ones often have to be protected from rogue clients. For most people, commissioning building work is not only a mammoth undertaking but also a giant step into the unknown, making them vulnerable to the blandishments of self-interested chancers taking advantage of their inexperience. The process is long, difficult and expensive, and there is plenty of opportunity for such people to appear along the way.

After three decades I feel I am just beginning to get the hang of it, and a quinquennial refresher of *The Honeywood File* and *The Honeywood Settlement* reminds me how lucky I am to have worked with the John Grigblays (and the Bloggses) of my profession. Anyone who has tried to fit a shelf, stood mystified in a DIY shop or waited in terror for the arrival of an emergency plumber will understand the tale, and anyone interested in reading or writing letters will enjoy the masterful way in which Cresswell has chosen to tell it.

GUS ALEXANDER set up his own practice in London in 1986 and has been working as an architect and writing about it ever since. He is currently completing an illustrated book of tales from the architect's life recorded in his own files.

This piece is one of the winning entries in our Older Writers' Competition.

The Supreme Diarist?

DEREK PARKER

At 20, mad about the theatre but living as far from Shaftesbury Avenue as you could get without tumbling into the Atlantic, I knew all about the latest productions in the West End. Moreover, I could have told you about Noël Coward's 1924 triumph with *The Vortex*, John Gielgud's 1935 shot at Romeo, and Olivier's 1944 stage triumph as Richard III.

This was courtesy of James Agate. Though he had died in 1947 I had many of his books of collected theatre criticism, from *Buzz Buzz* (1914) through *Brief Chronicles* (1943) to the wonderful evocation of musicals and light comedies, *Immoment Toys* (1945). It was some time, however, before I came across *Ego*, his diary, the first volume of which came out in 1932. In the first entry, he says that he started writing it 'because there seem to be a lot of things I want to say that other writers put into novels and accepted essayists into essays. Because it will be a relief to set down just what I do actually think, and in the first words to hand, instead of pondering what I *ought* to think and worrying about the words in which to express the hammered-out thought.' Rebecca West claimed that she would 'keep these journals as I keep the Goncourt Journals, as records of their time more truly historical than history', while in an obituary broadcast Alistair Cooke called Agate 'the supreme diarist'.

Agate's is a diary in the widest possible meaning of the word. He naturally records his daily activities, but he also sometimes includes letters he has written to the press and to his friends – and their

---

The nine volumes of James Agate's *Ego* (1932–47) are out of print.

replies. Very occasionally there will be a terse line, 'Dined with John [Gielgud], [Laurence] Olivier and Emlyn [Williams]' – but that will usually be followed by four pages of their conversation and followed up by the letters they exchanged next day carrying further the arguments they had had – about a play or an actor or a concert.

But first things first: I doubt whether any non-theatre-buff much under 50 is more than vaguely aware that someone called James Agate once existed. He was born in Manchester in 1877, the son of a linen draper – but a linen draper who was also prominent in the Manchester arts world: Mrs Agate was an accomplished pianist and Sarah Bernhardt came to dinner.

The boy went to Manchester Grammar School, but instead of university joined his father's business. In the early years of the new century he began writing theatre notices for the *Manchester Guardian*; but then came the war. He was already 37 but volunteered for service and was posted to France, whence he sent back to the *Guardian* a series of letters later published as *L. of C.* (Lines of Communication) which, though now forgotten, was regarded in its time as a classic of war literature. He married a French girl; but he was homosexual, and the marriage did not last – though he remained friends with his wife.

Back in England he set about his real career. Within a couple of years he had become theatre critic of the *Saturday Review* (a post previously held by both Bernard Shaw and Max Beerbohm), and in 1923 he moved to the *Sunday Times* where he remained until his death, the most influential British theatre critic. He published many volumes of collected criticism, which addicts of the genre continue to treasure. But it is the *Ego* series, covering the years 1932 to 1947, which anyone interested in English diaries should try to collect.

The diaries differ from most because despite what he wrote about putting down the first words that came to hand, in fact in the end he wrote his journal as carefully as he wrote anything else – something to which he confessed in *Ego 8*:

Shall I lose face if I confess that the *Ego* books are not the careless jottings of idle half-hours? That I think *Ego*, talk *Ego*, dream *Ego*? That I get up in the middle of the night to make a correction? That before the MS of any of my *Egos* reaches the publishers it has been through at least a dozen revisions? That it is only when the galley proofs arrive that the real work begins? I suppose that when I had finished with the galleys of *Ego 7* it would have been difficult to find fifty unaltered sentences . . . [and] actually I made over two thousand corrections on the page proofs of *Ego 7*.

He was meticulous about punctuation: 'Millais once confessed that the only thing he enjoyed about portrait painting was putting the highlights on the boots of his subjects; the only thing I really enjoy about writing is the punctuation.' He took infinite trouble: on one occasion, in May 1943, he wrote a notice of a play for the *Sunday Times*, 'went home, then decided the notice wasn't good enough: went down to the *ST* office, rescued the script, took it to the Café Royal, wrestled still further with it, took it back to the flat, and sat up till four still wrestling. The trouble with the thing was that there were too many words and too few ideas . . . Had another go this morning in the intervals of reading the week's books for the *Daily Express* . . . Shall doubtless have another go when the proofs arrive tomorrow. Who says I am not a spontaneous writer?'

A critic is surely nothing if he or she is not opinionated, and Agate needed no lesson from anyone about that. In the theatre he had no truck with 'producers', as directors were then called – he saw them merely as 'persons engaged by the management to conceal the fact that the players cannot act'. Writing to Tyrone Guthrie about his production of *Macbeth* in 1944:

If the producer thinks he can best interpret Shakespeare's woodland comedy by giving the fairies glass noses and sealing-wax ears I do not very much mind because in that instance production *is* the play . . . But I'm horribly annoyed when your highbrow producer makes a surrealist Lear emerge from a factory chimney wearing a stovepipe hat and using an umbrella to ward off, while apostrophising, the elements . . . What enrages me even more than his insanity is the pitiful ambition of the producer who must add his self-expression to his actor's, and so forces me to get my Shakespeare at two removes.

He loved to *épater*, and though the term 'politically correct' wasn't then in vogue, he certainly usually woke up in the morning with the idea of upsetting someone, and usually succeeded.

If I had my will, young girls would be taught nothing but cooking, sewing, and how to keep a house clean, and young boys no more than the trades by which they ultimately hope to support the young girls. This as to nineteen-twentieths of the youthful population. It would be left to the discretion of teachers to pick out the odd five per cent who can be educated. For note this. Before you can educate a mind you must have a mind to educate. It is a part of democratic cant to pretend that Nature has been fair and equitable in her distribution of mind. She has not; she has been infinitely capricious. Nineteen-twentieths of the population in this country has no more mind – I am not talking of soul – than a lamp-post.

He especially appreciated the advantage of upsetting the readers of the *Egos*. Among other things, this attracted an enormous amount of correspondence – with some correspondents, if they were sufficiently intelligent and witty, he would exchange letters for months, and for pages. These writers were often obscure, though he also corresponded voluminously with fellow authors and distinguished actors. His exchange of letters with George Lyttelton (later celebrated for his published correspondence with Rupert Hart-Davis) goes on spasmodically through the *Egos* for several years. Mrs Patrick Campbell

said: 'I did so enjoy your book. Everything that everybody writes in
it is so good.'

Witty himself, he was a provoker of wit in others, and a great
snapper-up of unconsidered trifles. An entry for 20 March 1934:

> To see Peter Page, laid up with gout and saying, 'I wish I had
> the pluck of old Lord K – I met him just before the last war,
> hobbling up the Haymarket. I hailed a cab and helped him in.
> He said "Thankee, m'boy. Tell the fellow to drive to Hyde Park
> Corner and stop at the first blonde."'

The *Egos* are full of small felicities. He was delighted for instance
to find a description of Southend in *The Tempest*:

> The approaching tide
> Will shortly fill the reasonable shore
> That now lies foul and muddy.

He saw everything through the prism of literature. There is a
sketch of the Rattenbury trial – the famous 1935 trial of Alma
Rattenbury for the murder (with her young lover) of her husband –
which he thought a living novel, the plot by Balzac. 'In the box Mrs
Rattenbury looked and talked exactly as I have always imagined
Emma Bovary looked and talked. Pure Flaubert . . . and there was
that part of her evidence in which she described how, trying to bring
her husband round, she first accidentally trod on his false teeth and
then tried to put them back into his mouth so that he could speak to
her. This was pure Zola.'

He was an extremely clubbable man – that was one of the reasons
for his incessant financial difficulties. He would keep a cab waiting
for hours while he dined his friends – always caviar and champagne,
of course (though on one occasion he noted that he only had enough
money for one half-bottle, so of course 'I drank it myself. One must
have a proper sense of self-esteem.').

He loved cricket and boxing, was a goodish golfer and a knowledgeable horse-fancier (he owned two Hackney show horses, both of them winners). He liked to dress the part, whether as a man-about-town or something different: in one *Ego*, 'Composed costume suitable for gent. on fine Sunday at Southend in April. Light blue shirt and collar, same colour stockings, violet and maroon tie, sporting small check jacket and waistcoat, Harris tweed plus fours large check, soft light-brown felt hat. Old brown shoes, nondescript handkerchief, and monocle.' (He asked his valet Fred, 'How do you like the *tout ensemble*?' Fred replied, 'Too much toot, and not enough of the other thing!')

James Agate died of heart disease in 1947, just after completing his ninth *Ego*. No one who enjoys diaries – from those of Pepys and Fanny Burney to Arnold Bennett's and Noël Coward's – can afford not to find even more room on their groaning shelves for the nine volumes of James Agate's *Ego*.

DEREK PARKER has one autograph note from James Agate, who offered in the *Daily Express* to comment on readers' writing. Aged 15, Parker sent in a short story. Agate wrote: 'Save your pennies and buy a decent typewriter – I can't read the stuff.'

When the Clock Struck Thirteen

MAGGIE FERGUSSON

A lot of the stories I loved most as a child involved doors. Aged about 4, I suppose, I passed through the small, latched door in the hillside, into Mrs Tiggywinkle's flagged kitchen, filled with the 'nice, hot, singey smell' of ironing, busy and reassuring. A few years later came the doors into Narnia, the Secret Garden and Wonderland, Bilbo Baggins's 'perfectly round' green door with its shiny yellow brass knob 'in the exact middle', the door into the Yellow Dwarf's home in the orange tree, and the dark door into Bluebeard's bloody chamber.

Several years on again – looking now towards the end of school, and the wider world – I remember the thrill of reading about Charles Ryder's early days at Oxford, and his 'faint, unrecognized apprehension that here, at last, I should find that low door in the wall, which others, I knew, had found before me, which opened on an enclosed and enchanted garden, which was somewhere, not overlooked by any window, in the heart of that great city'.

But reading to my own children, the door I've been happiest to pass through again is the door into Tom's Midnight Garden – a door one can only imagine because, unlike most of the others, it is never described.

The plot of Philippa Pearce's classic novel for children is simple. Tom Long, a boy of about 10, in quarantine for measles, is dispatched to spend the summer holidays with his childless uncle and aunt. They are a dreary couple – Alan Kitson, ponderous, literal-minded,

Philippa Pearce, *Tom's Midnight Garden* (1958)
OUP · Pb · 240pp · £6.99 · ISBN 9780192792426

quick-tempered; his wife, Gwen, kindly but cowed, and claustro-phobically doting. Because of the danger of infection, Tom is forbidden even to answer the door to the milkman, but instead remains cooped up inside the Kitsons' poky flat – one of a number of apartments carved awkwardly out of what was once a large Victorian house.

In an attempt to cheer him up, Aunt Gwen cooks enormous meals, swimming in sauces ('whipped cream and rum butter and real mayonnaise'), which cause Tom to toss and turn in bed, sullen and wakeful. One night, unable to sleep, he counts as the grandfather clock in the hall strikes thirteen. Creeping down to investigate, he opens the back door that normally leads to a strip of paving and some communal dustbins, and finds himself instead in a beautiful, rambling summer garden.

The garden is there, waiting for him as the clock strikes thirteen, every night, and in it he meets a little girl, Hatty, an orphan ward who is, like him, lonely and in need of a friend. Together, night after night, they play in the garden, climbing trees, making bows and arrows, wandering among the cacti and the creepers in the green-house, breathing in the warm, stifling air. Occasionally they argue, and when they do it is almost always about which of them is real, and which a ghost. But the arguments blow away like thistledown: Tom and Hatty need one another so badly that they cannot afford to dwell on the oddness of their friendship.

For Tom, the summer holidays march forwards, day by day, in a conventional manner. But in the garden, though it is almost always summer, time dances about. If one night Hatty is a girl of about Tom's age, the next he finds her a tiny, newly orphaned child, dressed in black, weeping for her parents. And sometimes she is almost grown up. On Tom's final visit, she is about to be married, and because she no longer needs his friendship, he has become insub-stantial, almost invisible to her.

The night before he returns home to his parents, Tom creeps

downstairs to find the bolt to the back door rusted and immovable, and the garden gone. I won't spoil things by revealing the final, bittersweet twist to the tale; but it makes for the most moving ending to any children's book I know.

There is everything here to keep a child of 8 or 9 absorbed. The chapters are not too long – about right for a quarter of an hour's bedtime reading. Each ends with some conundrum or catch of the breath to draw you into the next; each, in the original 1958 edition, opens with a detailed line-drawing by Susan Einzig, the brilliant children's illustrator who arrived on one of the last Kindertransport trains to reach Britain before the outbreak of war. And woven through the story – though never outweighing the excitement – is a thread of the kind of sadness children relish, once it begins to dawn on them that life is not always straightforward.

But what amazed me, when I read the book to my own children, was how much it has to offer grown-ups too. I'd been prompted to take it off the shelf by meeting someone who had known the author well, and was able to tell me a bit about the circumstances in which the book was written. Philippa Pearce was the youngest of four children. Her father was a miller and corn merchant whose family had lived for three generations in the Mill House on the upper reaches of the river Cam, near the village of Great Shelford. When, his children grown up, he came to sell the house, Philippa decided to capture her childhood memories of the walled garden where she, and her father and grandfather before her, had played as children.

No amount of research could have enabled a writer to make a garden so completely real for her readers, and Pearce's love of the place is shot through every detail – from the muslin bags muffling the pears to prevent bruising to the baby frogs who hide under the strawberry leaves; from the shadowy tunnel between the yew trees and the nut stubs to the gooseberry nets from which Tom and Hatty release trapped blackbirds, to the Sensitive Plant that cowers in the greenhouse and shrinks, on stroking, 'in one droop of nervous dejection'.

Susan Einzig

Pearce draws on her father's memories as well as her own. He had told her about how, during the great frost of 1895, he and his friends skated down the Cam. In the book's most memorable chapter Tom and Hatty skate together one winter's afternoon, under frozen willows and past ice-locked boats, all the way to Ely. As the sun is about to set, they climb 286 steps to the top of the cathedral tower, and look out across the fens. It is their last great adventure. Hatty is nearly 20 by now, and on the point of getting engaged. To her Tom is becoming increasingly tenuous. 'I wasn't sure if it were you', she admits, 'or a trick of the frostlight.'

Philippa Pearce was nearly 40 when she wrote the book, and hand in hand with her pin-sharp child's-eye recall goes the kind of wisdom that only comes when a person is able to look back over a good chunk of life. She understands, for example, about providence – how what present themselves, at first, as crushing disasters often bring unlooked-for blessings; how the best things come unbidden. The first chapter of the book is heavy with Tom's disappointment that his summer holidays have been ruined. He had planned to build a tree house with his brother, Peter, in the little apple tree in their ribbon of suburban garden. He *does* build a tree house, a grander one than could ever have fitted in an apple tree, with Hatty, in the branches of a great yew tree called the Steps of St Paul's. I was reminded, rereading the book, of a passage towards the end of George Mackay Brown's autobiography, *For the Islands I Sing*. There are, Brown says, two wills at work in every life – the personal will and 'another will that we have no control over . . . It "prevents us everywhere", as Eliot says, but it also offers opportunities beyond anything we could have hoped for.' Philippa Pearce would have liked that, I think.

I was reminded, too, of a striking detail in the closing chapter of Artemis Cooper's biography of Patrick Leigh Fermor. Before he died, Fermor chose as the reading at his funeral a passage from the Apocryphal Book of St James describing 'a moment when time stands still'. That, in a way, is what Philippa Pearce does here – she stops time in its tracks by trapping her memories between the pages of a book, like pressed flowers. But she does more than this. Time, in *Tom's Midnight Garden*, does not stand still, but bends and twists so that past and present embrace and comfort one another. The story revolves around two children, Hatty and Tom; but between Hatty's late Victorian childhood and Tom's in the 1950s lay two world wars. I wonder whether there was, at the back of Philippa Pearce's mind as she wrote, a desire to build a kind of rainbow bridge across those decades of devastation?

So how does one categorize this small masterpiece? It's not quite memoir and not entirely make-believe. It's almost as if, in writing it, Philippa Pearce was offering her own mysterious postscript to those beautiful verses from Ecclesiastes. There's a time to be born, and a time to die; a time to mourn, and a time to dance; a time to keep, and a time to cast away. And there's a time, perhaps, when time itself curls about, accommodates, suspends its own iron laws for a while, to help us on our way.

MAGGIE FERGUSSON, who has written biographies of George Mackay Brown and Michael Morpurgo, divides her working life between the Royal Society of Literature and the *Economist* magazine *Intelligent Life*.

Pox Britannica

SUE GEE

In November 1922, George Orwell (or Eric Blair, as he was then) arrived in Burma, to take up a post with the Indian Imperial Police. He was 19, not long out of Eton, which he had attended on a scholarship; his family could not afford to send him to university. He moved about: from hill station to frontier outpost, to the outskirts of Rangoon, eventually posted to the town of Katha, in Upper Burma. It was on this remote place that he based the town of Kyauktada, the setting for his first novel, *Burmese Days*. It was published in New York by Harper & Brothers in 1934, and then, in 1935, in London, by Victor Gollancz, who had – needlessly – been afraid of libel.

In 1934, my father, aged 22, arrived in the province of Bihar, in northern India. For five years he was to supervise the large district of a sugar plantation before serving in the Indian Army until the end of the war. This tenuous temporal connection between two utterly different men is what set me reading *Burmese Days*.

In my twenties I had read almost all of Orwell except, for no good reason, this novel. Decades later, steeped in my father's tape-recorded stories of his time in India, and trying to write my own novel about the aftermath of his colonial experience, I was reading all things relevant, from Forster to Rushdie – and then, almost as an afterthought, Orwell. Everyone should read this novel, I think now.

Much darker than Forster, whose *A Passage to India* was published ten years earlier, and whose knowledge of India was as a gentle

George Orwell, *Burmese Days* (1934)
Penguin · Pb · 320pp · £9.99 · ISBN 9780141185378

traveller, *Burmese Days* describes a country of ravishing beauty and squalor, with an intolerable climate, in which there is corruption in every sweating pore. And although it offers an unflinching portrait of the casual – and deliberate – cruelties of colonialism, its villain is Burmese. It burns with a clear-sighted anger, exploring all aspects of people and place in empire's waning days – most poignantly through the complex character of Flory, a lonely timber merchant who both loathes and loves the country, and who understands its culture as no one among the yellowing old bores in the Club will do. It is he who strikes a plangent note on his enforced return from an attempted visit to England: unexpectedly, he is glad to be back, knows that this is his home. What he longs for is someone to share it with, and in this he is doomed.

Set in a ring of hills, Kyauktada is a railway town lying between jungle and the banks of the Irrawaddy. Orwell drew a little map of it: the Club and the hospital on the river; the seething jail where men are flogged and hanged; the maidan where polo is played; the tin-roofed church; the slender tower of the pagoda rising from a grove of peepal trees; the bazaar, with its shouts and smells and prostitutes. Vultures soar and circle in the heat.

Close to the hospital is the house of Dr Veraswami, who aspires to be elected the first non-European member of the Club. Nearby lives U Po Kyin, the obese and murderous Sub-divisional Magistrate of Kyauktada. As the novel opens, he is sitting on his veranda, chewing betel from a lacquered box and thinking about his past life.

As 'a naked, pot-bellied child' he had watched the victory march of British troops into Mandalay, and in his awe and terror had conceived his ambition: to fight on their side, to become a parasite upon them. Through 'a lucky stroke of blackmail', through theft, bribery and betrayal, he has risen to power. Now, all his energies have one aim: the downfall of Dr Veraswami. 'We are going to slander him, destroy his reputation and destroy him for ever,' he tells his servant. 'It will be a rather delicate operation.' And then it is *he* who will be elected to 'the European Club, that remote, mysterious temple, that holy of holies far harder of entry than Nirvana!'

On the other side of the town, facing the jungle, lie the houses of some of the British: Macgregor, the Deputy Commissioner and Club Secretary; the Lackersteens, he the alcoholic director of a timber firm, she his discontented wife; and Flory, Veraswami's friend.

Flory lives with his mildewed books, his dog and Ko S'la, the servant he has had since his arrival. Ma Hla May, his doll-like mistress, is a frequent visitor, a young woman he uses for sex, though it leaves him disgusted and ashamed. What marks him out, what has in some ways formed his character, is a dark blue birthmark, stretching down his left cheek. 'He was quite aware of its hideousness.'

Educated and bullied at a 'cheap, third-rate public school' he has through solitary reading broadened his mind, but there is only Veraswami, kindly and put upon, Anglophile to the last cell of his body, with whom to debate ideas. Dr Veraswami has a passionate admiration for the English which a thousand snubs from Englishmen have not shaken, and Flory's seditious opinions shock him. 'At least you have brought us law and order. The unswerving British justice and the Pax Britannica.' To which Flory replies, 'Pox Britannica, doctor . . . Of course I don't deny that we modernize this country in certain ways . . . In fact, before we've finished we'll have wrecked the whole Burmese national culture.'

Meanwhile, there is outrage at the Club. In response to a government edict, Macgregor has proposed that a non-European member should be elected. 'I suppose you'd like little Veraswami for a Club member, eh?' demands Ellis, a timber firm assistant, of Flory. 'That pot-bellied, greasy little sod of a nigger doctor . . . I'll die in the ditch before I see a nigger in here.'

Flory is unable to meet his eyes. And later he weakly signs a letter of disagreement with the proposal. 'He had done it for the same reason as he had done a thousand such things in his life; because he lacked the small spark of courage that was needed to refuse.'

Soon afterwards, he receives an anonymous letter, warning him against Dr Veraswami, 'NOT A GOOD MAN, in no ways a worthy friend of European gentlemen'. As he tears it to pieces, he hears sudden screams from the jungle – 'an English voice, a woman's, crying out in terror'. Racing with his dog towards the sound, he discovers a young woman in terror of a buffalo, which he quickly scares away.

And here they are: a lonely, middle-aged man with a hideous birthmark, and the slender 20-year-old niece of the Lackersteens, fresh from Paris. Elizabeth has cropped hair, a delicate, oval face and blue eyes as pale as harebells. She is full of gratitude for her rescue; as they walk back, and stop to look at the flowers in his garden, a pang of unreasonable happiness goes through them both.

What follows is utterly compelling: an account of the rise and fall of love – and never were two people more ill-suited – interwoven, in the interminable heat, with the treacherous and inexorable machinations of U Po Kyin. They culminate in the arrival at the Club one evening of a murderous mob.

It is Flory, acting at last, who saves the day, but the reigniting of Elizabeth's affections lasts only until U Po Kyin's last vile act, and from that moment all meaning in his life is gone.

What is on show in this flawlessly constructed novel is the ways in which colonialism destroys itself. At its worst, it devalues 'native' culture while almost inevitably sowing aspiration and ambition for something it will never give: equality. Thwarted, that ambition turns against it – or, in the case of U Po Kyin, brings tragedy to good men.

Amid passages of great descriptive beauty, Orwell's dry, ironic voice charts events which end quite terribly. And then he swings the whole thing round: terrible acts, and shallow people – oh, how shallow is Elizabeth! – are rewarded with status and power. The villain is destined for glory. And this is empire.

'Indian Refugees from Burma', the only poem SUE GEE's father ever wrote, appears in her new novel, *Coming Home*, published in August.

The Heart's Affections

VICTORIA NEUMARK

I was 17 when I finished reading the letters of John Keats for the first time. It was a warm summer evening and I was lying in bed with the volume I'd chosen, rather at random, for my school's Soulsby Prize in English 1967–8 – as the bookplate tells me today.

Tears poured down my face. I ran to my mother's bedroom. 'Mum, Mum, Keats is dead! He's dead.' I sat on her bed. She looked up from her thriller. 'Well darling, it was a long time ago,' she said mildly.

My father had died the year before. I daresay that may have muted the impact of Keats's demise for her. But for me, who had steadfastly refused to think about my father's death, preferring to concentrate on English literature and a possible escape route to Oxford, it was overwhelming. He was so young, he was so loveable, his poetry was so full of life. Above all, he was so real. How could he be dead?

Tears still come to my eyes as I read the final letters in Frederick Page's 1954 selection for Oxford University Press. In 1821 Keats, not yet 26, was dying and far from home, having just produced some stunning poetry yet never having made love to his sweetheart, Fanny Brawne. He writes, wrenchingly, to his friend Brown, 'I should have had her when I was in health and I should have remained well. I can bear to die – I cannot bear to leave her.'

Of course, I now know that there are other letters which Page did not select, showing Keats in an altogether more lusty light; that Keats

Jon Mee and Robert Gittings (eds.), *John Keats: Selected Letters* (2009)
OUP · Pb · 480pp · £9.99 · ISBN 9780199555734
Frederick Page's selection of Keats's letters (1954) is out of print.

had probably had sexual relations at least once, even if not with his true love; that the world is monstrously unfair in more ways than the deaths of youthful poets. But I still weep for Keats, even though I have now seen two of my sons pass the age at which he died.

The story of the letters opens in 1816 when Keats, nearly 21 and living with his two brothers in rented rooms in London, writes to Charles Cowden Clarke, son of the headmaster of Clarke's School, where Keats had had a happy education. Keats is writing to tease his old friend into honouring a promise to introduce him to Leigh Hunt. Gatekeeper to a literary Bohemia, Hunt was to be an important mentor and promoter for Keats, whom he straightaway christened 'Junkets'.

'Junkets' – that hit the nail on the head. Keats's letters overflow with sensual delight: in 'books, fruit, french wine and fine whether [*sic*] and a little music out of doors'; in 'wandering as free as a stag' about the countryside with his mates; in punning and jokes and rude, dashed-off doggerel; in intoxicated immersion in experience. 'I can never feel certain of any truth but from a clear perception of its Beauty,' he writes.

Letters were as fashionable a medium of expression then as Twitter is now. Keats often writes, particularly to his younger sister Fanny, about 'crossing' (to save postage, charged by the sheet, people would write crosswise over their own words), about how to pick up letters in strange towns, about getting his letters copied so that she can read about his travels. These are letters to entertain, to share gossip and news.

Yet these merry, sparkling accounts of tea parties, theatre trips, dinners, walks and visits to friends bespeak more than a young man's fun. Keats does nothing by halves. He gives up medicine in favour of the poetic vocation, fuelled by admiration for Wordsworth and, famously, Chapman's version of Homer. He lives beyond his slender means with rueful, intense hopes of his ship coming in – with a new play, with journalism, with an epic poem.

And, of course, he falls in love. Women are a marvel to him and, reading between the lines, he was magnetically attractive to them. Not just to Fanny Brawne, but to the sisters of his friend Reynolds, to the wife of his friend Charles Dilke, to his own sister and sister-in-law, Leigh Hunt's whole circle: all fuss over him and pet him.

But there was another side. 'I must choose between despair and Energy – I choose the latter,' he writes to a woman friend. Mood swings were intensified by misfortunes. Their skinflint guardian imposed mean conditions on the four orphaned Keats children – John, George, Tom and Fanny. Money and emotion were expended on lawsuits, which grated on Keats's over-sensitive nature. What he called his 'lunes' led him to fall out with good and influential friends like Hunt and the painter Benjamin Haydon. He was so close to his next brother, George, that he resented George and his wife Georgiana emigrating to America in 1818 and reproached them for it, though still filling his letters with affectionate family banter. On top of this turmoil, Tom Keats fell sick and died of TB not long after George and Georgiana had left.

Though this tragedy was ultimately John's own death warrant, it was also the crucible for his writing. Struggling to nurse Tom – 'his identity presses on me so all day that I am obliged to go out' – a 'fever' of sorrow accelerated his maturity. His words burst off the page. 'Do you not see how necessary a World of Pains and troubles is to school an Intelligence and make it a Soul?'

In a flood of letters accompanying Tom's death, Keats pondered on poetry – that particular state of poetic receptivity he called 'negative capability' – on love and life. All day and night in 1819 he inhaled scientific and scholarly sources, building, as he described it in the 'Ode to Psyche', the 'wreath'd trellis of a working brain'. 'I am', he wrote, 'a little more of a Philosopher than I was, consequently a little less of a versifying Pet Lamb.'

These letters are masterly prose, matching the great Odes of his final writing year, 1819. So many passages leap to the eye – underlined by 17-year-old me in shaky red biro in my little blue volume. 'I am certain of nothing but the Holiness of the Heart's affections and the Truth of the Imagination . . . I have never yet been able to perceive how anything can be known for truth by consecutive reasoning . . . O for a life of sensation rather than of thoughts!'

Surely, it is only a thinking person who calls for sensation over thought. But perhaps Keats meant what he said when he wrote to his sister Fanny: 'Do not suffer your Mind to dwell upon unpleasant reflections – that sort of thing has been the destruction of my health.' Jealousy became an agony. He could shrug off negative reviews and snide comments. But how to give up what and whom you love? 'How astonishingly does the sense of leaving the natural world impress a sense of its beauties upon us.'

But a few short years divide Keats's first gleeful dive into the – then as now – shark-infested waters of literary London from his coughing out his lungs in a rented room in Rome. Although, as I read these letters now, they are haunted by a sense of the end, they still pulse with life.

He woos his girl, by fair means and foul:

I have never known any unalloy'd Happiness for many days together: the death or sickness of some one has always spoilt my hours – and now when none such troubles oppress me, it is you must confess very hard that another sort of pain should haunt me . . . Will you confess this in the Letter you must write immediately and do all you can do to console me in it – make it rich as a draught of poppies to intoxicate me – write the softest words and kiss them that I may at least touch my lips where yours have been.

He jokes with his sister. 'I admire lolling on a lawn by a water-lilied pond to eat white currants and see goldfish: and go to the fair in the evening if I'm good. There is not hope for that – one is sure to get into some mess before evening.'

He begs for money from his publisher; he congratulates friends on getting married; he marvels at scenery – 'I live in the eye, and the imagination, surpassed, is at rest' – and broods on unfairness. 'The first thing that strikes me on hearing a misfortune having befallen another is this – "Well, it cannot be helped: he will have the pleasure of trying the resources of his spirit."' In all of this, he is intensely alive: pugnacious, funny and clear-eyed.

In that final year, 1820–1, Keats became wise beyond his years. His writing, finally confined to letters after poetry became unattainable, tore away all flim-flam from the process of dying.

> I have been well, healthy, alert &c, walking with her – and now – the knowledge of contrast, feeling for light and shade, all that information (primitive sense) necessary for a poem are great enemies to the recovery of the stomach. There, you rogue, I put you to the torture – but you must bring your philosophy to bear – as I do mine, really – or how should I be able to live?

His farewell is gallant. 'I can scarcely bid you good bye even in a letter. I always made an awkward bow.'

How can Keats be dead? I can hear him. And his voice still makes me cry.

VICTORIA NEUMARK is still struggling to make sense of life. As well as the letters of Keats, she finds that France, Shakespeare and gardening are a help. Not forgetting the holiness of the heart's affections and a glass of red wine with beaded bubbles winking at the brim.

Auburn in Wartime

URSULA BUCHAN

I came across *The Oaken Heart* quite by chance when I was scouring the history shelves in the University Library in Cambridge, looking for memoirs that might add colour and depth to my book on gardening in the Second World War. I had heard of Margery Allingham, of course, and had read *The Tiger in the Smoke* as a teenager, but I had no idea that she had written an account of her life in the Essex village of Tolleshunt D'Arcy between July 1938 and May 1941. This was a stroke of luck: to find a proper writer (with a large garden and a gardener) who could honestly and clear-sightedly anatomize her feelings and sensations, and quote those of her neighbours, during the Munich crisis, the great evacuation of children and mothers to the country when war broke out, the retreat from Dunkirk, the Battle of Britain and the London Blitz.

Margery Allingham wrote the book because her American publisher thought his people would want to know what was happening to British civilians and perhaps be more inclined to come to their aid. With her artist husband, Philip Youngman Carter, she had lived in a large and handsome Queen Anne house in the centre of the village (which she calls Auburn) since 1935, but she had been born in rural Essex and knew its quirky people intimately. Nevertheless, it is possible to discern – particularly at the beginning of the book – her understandable nervousness about describing her neighbours and

Margery Allingham, *The Oaken Heart: The Story of an English Village at War* (1941)
Golden Duck · Pb · 384p · £13.99 · ISBN 9781899262038

friends and generalizing about their
reactions, but she does it with such
skill and affection that I should be
surprised if any of them were mor-
tally offended (although there will
always be one or two in any village
who 'take agin'). Certainly the presence of dozens of signatures of village
inhabitants at the back of the edition
I read suggests that most of them
must have taken it in good part.

P. Youngman Carter

And why not, because the prose is warmed by the affection and
admiration she obviously felt for Tolleshunt D'Arcy and its people,
at a time when a village of 600 souls was still almost self-sufficient
and had a very particular identity, different even from its near neighbours. The village boasted a blacksmith's forge, shops, pubs and
farms, and most of the inhabitants had lived there all their lives.
Margery does not attempt to idealize them or hide their foibles but
she does hint at their quiet courage and stoicism, caught as they were
in a very inconvenient place so close to the North Sea.

Margery's house became the Air Raid Precautions and First Aid
post as well as a billet for the officers of successive battalions of soldiers on invasion watch. A strip of her meadow became a soldier's
camp, but only a strip, so that the hay could still be cut. And she was
closely involved in organizing the finding of homes for 275 evacuees
who arrived so precipitately and, in many cases, so disastrously in
early September 1939. (This book is a cool antidote to the often soft-
focused memoirs of evacuees which line the social history shelves in
bookshops.) Meanwhile, as the village waited to be bombed or worse,
she was still spending several hours a day writing an Albert Campion
detective story (*Traitor's Purse*), for she always needed to earn money.

In *The Oaken Heart*, Margery carefully examines her motives, her
fears, her hopes and her reactions, and her fascination at the way in

which wartime conditions drew disparate people together in often unexpected ways. She prods her psyche for signs of weakness or cowardice. There is a particularly striking passage when she looks around at her neighbours listening to a scarifying lecture in the village hall on what would happen if the Germans dropped poison gas bombs.

> Half-way through, when P.Y.C. (who was acting as a sort of lecturer's stooge) was being shown exactly how to make an airlock entrance, and my mind was running over the suitability of various old curtains on the top shelf of the linen cupboard, I suddenly saw the abyss at our feet as vividly as if I had looked over the side of a house. To realise is one thing but to see is another and I saw that they were talking about a corrosive poison to be sprayed over one civilised people by what was presumed to be another. I wondered if we were all insane and so nearly squeaked aloud . . . that I felt the blood rushing into my face with embarrassment . . . I looked around me furtively to see if I had been noticed and saw all the well-known faces turned gravely towards the stage.

Striking too is the village's dismay when Belgium surrenders and the French give up on Paris, as well as its sourness at not being close enough to the sea to send 'little ships' across the Channel to Dunkirk.

For historians, this kind of memoir is beyond price because it is contemporary. Without foreknowledge of what tomorrow or next year will bring, the emotions Margery describes are genuine, especially the see-sawing between hope and despair, the need to show a brave face to the world when everyone is watching everyone else for signs of weakness, and the desire to draw comfort from the small, everyday things which had once been taken for granted. The memoir was finished a month before the Germans turned on Russia, so before the threat of invasion finally receded.

In the process of describing life in Essex in 1940, she reveals a deeply innocent England that has now comprehensively disappeared, seen in the peculiarly intense light of wartime experience. For example, she tells the tale of how colonial soldiers (many of whom were based in Essex) waggishly swapped all the babies around in the pram park behind Woolworths in the nearest town and how this story amused Tolleshunt D'Arcy. We can scarcely now imagine a time when people felt that they might safely leave their babies unattended while they went shopping.

Since I first found a copy of this book, a new edition has been published by Golden Duck, with a characteristically wise and reflective foreword by Ronald Blythe, and a helpful introduction and notes by Margery's biographer, Julia Jones. From the notes I discovered – to my fascination, for I had had no idea – that my stepmother's parents had been part of the Tolleshunt D'Arcy story. This edition also includes extracts from Margery's diaries for the period, which clearly show the tension she felt in combining her many wartime duties with writing.

All in all, however, Margery's wartime experiences seem to have been salutary. The Youngman Carters, in their mid-thirties, were part of a disillusioned generation, children during the Great War who had lost their belief in the things their parents had cared about. The tumultuous, terrifying and tremendous events of 1940 beat that out of them. Margery's relief is obvious. The book ends with the words:

> What a period! What an age to be alive in!
> Oh, thank God I was born when I was.

URSULA BUCHAN's latest book, *A Green and Pleasant Land: How England's Gardeners Fought the Second World War*, has just been published.

Three in a Bed

YSENDA MAXTONE GRAHAM

'Where are we, exactly?'

That is a question I've asked all too often. The scene: three in a bed (husband, 11-year-old son in the middle, me); dog asleep at the foot. The time: 9.30 p.m. The reason: husband is reading aloud to us, and last night, as usual, I fell asleep towards the end of the chapter. Surely the most delicious kind of falling asleep is the gentle, helpless drifting off you do to the sound of the reading voice.

The son is slightly exasperated at this question as he never falls asleep while being read to. On the contrary, he changes position, kicks out, laughs, comments and speculates about what's going to happen next. The story activates rather than lulls him.

'Mummy! Honestly! Don't you remember? They've just arrived at Helm's Deep.'

Of course. Helm's Deep. But just hearing those words brings on this evening's overwhelming sleepiness. Théoden. Denethor. What exactly is the difference between those two? Husband and son know; mother is not so sure.

'Tell the Éored to assemble on the path, and make ready to ride the Entwade!'

Mmm? You've lost me again, but it all sounds lovely.

With one of our older sons, my husband walked the 155-mile London Loop round the wooded edges of the metropolis, which took half a year of Saturdays. Reading *The Lord of the Rings* aloud to the youngest is the stationary equivalent of such a journey: a time-consuming adventure in which the partakers share every knoll and tussock. The nightly habit of reading aloud has become something the family depends on for equilibrium. Whatever happens in the husband's stressful job; whatever happens in the son's school day; whatever worries we all have, we know that before bedtime we will walk together into the world of a story we don't want to end.

Just as he prefers to drive rather than be driven, my husband would rather read aloud than be read to. Both preferences suit me fine as I hate getting back into the original lane after overtaking and I get a sore throat after two pages of reading aloud. Over the past year he has read the whole *Lord of the Rings* trilogy, followed by *Watership Down*, followed by the *Odyssey* in the E. V. Rieu translation. Each book has brought different delights and challenges.

In *The Lord of the Rings*, one of the challenges is how to tackle the songs. You come across songs without warning in Tolkien's books: turn a page and you're face to face with a long wad of italics divided (or sometimes not) into verses. You must quickly gauge whether this is a minor-key song (about loss) or a major-key one (about merry feasts) and invent a tune accordingly. And, having invented it, you must remember it and repeat it in the next verse: a feat not made easier by the vocabulary Tolkien throws at you: 'O Orofané, Lassemista, Carnimíre . . .' Sometimes, when extremely yawny after a tough day of wrangling with Los Angeles lawyers, Michael has been known to substitute 'he said' for 'he sang' at the beginning and hope nobody notices. Occasionally, Tolkien unhelpfully writes, 'Thus Gandalf softly sang' *after* a song is over, by which time it's too late to sing it.

Imagined worlds work especially well as read-aloud books. You step together into a magical landscape. I must say, though, when Tolkien is being read aloud, it can sometimes be a bit like doing a long communal Rambler's Association trail in walking boots. Thousands upon thousands of words are devoted to the terrain. Tolkien never allows you to forget whether his characters are trudging downhill or uphill. If I've heard one 'The western side of each ridge was steep and difficult, but the eastern slopes were gentler, furrowed with many gullies and narrow ravines', I've heard a million.

What the reader-aloud, and the read-to, look forward to most is when characters make remarks in their own entirely distinctive fashion. That's when the son roars with laughter and bounces around ('Keep *still*, can't you?'). And that's when the accents and voices come in. Every British man, I suppose, has his armoury of accents and voices he can 'do'. In Michael's case, the accents include Yorkshire, West Country, West Indian, Germanic, Morningside, Glaswegian, Brummy and Cockney. The voices include military-posh, school-master-disdainful, grandfatherly, regal, 'noble, good and true', boyish and (for girls) either girlish-innocent or tomboy. He tends to do baddies in schoolmaster-disdainful, and saves the 'noble, good and true' voice for the hero. Again, the reader-aloud has to get these accents and voices right first time – rather as *Private Eye* has to find a new self-parody form for a Prime Minister as soon as a new one is elected. Once you've decided on it, you're stuck with it. (The 'St Albion Parish News' never was as good as 'Dear Bill'.)

Just as pianists say you can't hide when you're playing Mozart, and actors say you can't hide when you're doing radio, authors know they can't hide when their books are being read aloud. Their stylistic bumps and infelicities are simultaneously aired and shared. Tolkien can get a bit Biblical. 'And Aragorn looked on the slain, and he said, "Here lie men that are not the folk of Mordor."' But he's a master of Latinate-avoiding English, and his Anglo-Saxon prose is music to the sleepy ears.

The Lord of the Rings was always going to be a hard act to follow. There was a sense of bereavement when the trilogy was finished – more so, perhaps, than after a solitary reading, because it was shared and because more physical effort had been put into it. Michael decided on *Watership Down* which he had loved as a boy. The thick Puffin book sat unread on my bookshelf for years because as a child I couldn't bear long descriptions of nature, and the novel (in my mind) made the mistake of beginning with the sentence 'The primroses were over', and then proceeded to give us two slab-like paragraphs describing ragwort, a brook, a brambly ditch, king-cups, watercress, a blackbird and a warren at peace.

The book is in fact a masterpiece. If only I'd got through that first page as a girl, I would have met Hazel and Fiver on page 2. Richard Adams's chapters are shorter than Tolkien's – five to ten pages rather than fifteen to twenty. Short chapters are a good thing for bedtime reading. The reader-aloud can conclude the evening's business with the words, 'And here ends Chapter 9', rather than having to say at an arbitrary moment, 'Well, we'd better stop there. You really must go to bed. No, you really must or you'll be exhausted. We'll read the rest of the chapter tomorrow, OK?'

Adams, like Tolkien, has dreamed up a profoundly imagined alternative world into which the reader-aloud and the read-to can step together. Decades of thought about what it would really be like to be a rabbit must have gone into the book's creation. That was another thing that put me off as a child: the illustration of a large, staring rabbit on the front cover. Did I really want to know what it must be like to be a rabbit? Let alone get to know an invented rabbit-language called Lapine?

I now see that the world Adams created illuminates the lives of not only rabbits but all of us, illustrating how humans (as well as rabbits) can create both communal paradises and communal hells. After reading it you care deeply about your fellow living beings, whether human or animal. The vocabulary of Lapine is wholly convincing. A tractor is a 'hrududu'. 'Frith' is the sun, i.e. God to rabbits. Noon is 'ni-frith'. To feed is to silflay. Enemy animals are 'elil'. The 11-year-old was enchanted by all this.

As for the voices and accents, the character we most looked forward to hearing was Keehar, the outspoken black-headed gull who befriends and helps the rabbits. Viennese-West Indian seems to be the accent Adams had in mind, going by the spellings. 'You 'urt me? I 'urt you like dam.' Of Bigwig, 'Meester Pigvig, 'e plenty good fella.' And of the central quest of the book, which is to find some does to come and live with the rabbits, 'Vind finish, den I fly. Fly for you. Find plenty mudders, tell you vere dey are, ya?'

There's an adorable (though not of key importance to the plot) mouse whom the rabbits rescue from certain death. The grateful mouse, speaking 'in the simple *lingua franca* of the hedgerow', says, 'You 'elp a mouse. One time a mouse 'elp a you.' We yelped with delight when we heard that. It was about the sweetest thing we'd ever heard a fictional animal say. When a book is read aloud, you do notice and share its unimportant nooks and crannies, and this is another joy.

Did you notice that word 'does'? Of course, it's the plural of 'doe' rather than the third-person singular of 'to do' – but the reader-aloud can be tripped up by that kind of thing. Michael was not sure how to pronounce the name of the chief baddie, General Woundwort. He plumped for 'wound' as past participle of 'wind', thinking of bindweed. Actually, I think it should be 'wound' as in 'injury', as woundwort turns out to be a 'wound-healing herb'. But it was too late to change, once we'd found this out.

In the next book, the *Odyssey*, we became unnecessarily interested in a character called Thoon. On suddenly coming across this name in the list of Phaeacians competing at the Games, Michael pronounced the name to rhyme with 'spoon'. On reflection, he supposed the 'o's should be separate, as in 'oology'. But – as with Woundwort – once pronounced, too late to change, and we elevated and speculated endlessly on this very minor character. (That was in fact Thoon's sole mention.) There was another name which, again, one might not have noticed if reading the book to oneself, but which, read aloud, was bound to become a favourite, and that was Antiphates. Reading that name aloud to a prep-school-age boy is asking for trouble, and from that moment on, the poor man's name was never mentioned without a made-up accompaniment of Homeric epithets: Antiphates, the wind-breaker, arriving with a thunderous clatter.

Anna Trench

'Dawn, fresh and rosy-fingered'. How many times did we hear that? Countless times. At first, fearing that the 11-year-old might tire of this repeated epithet, Michael left one or two of them out and just said 'dawn'. But of course the boy loved the repetitions, and started chanting them aloud, along with the reader. 'When they had satisfied their hunger and their thirst . . .'

To step into the world of the *Odyssey* is particularly delicious after a hard day in the twenty-first-century office or school. First, a slave brings you a silver basin in which to rinse your hands, and then he rubs you with oil. Then the faithful housekeeper mixes you some mellow wine and pours it into a gold cup, and sets before you some bread and a choice of delicacies. Domestic palace life is blissfully well described in the *Odyssey* – you wish you were there – and it comes as a terrible shock at the end when Odysseus massacres all the suitors in an orgy of blood and guts. I'm not sure we can face the *Iliad* after that horror. We've decided on the Philip Pullman trilogy instead.

YSENDA MAXTONE GRAHAM is the author of *Mr Tibbits's Catholic School* and *The Real Mrs Miniver*, both Slightly Foxed Editions.

Bibliography

Coming attractions . . .

RICHARD MABEY finds a cellmate

ANNE BOSTON falls for Carrington

MARK HAWORTH-BOOTH returns to Kettle's Yard

JANE RIDLEY curtseys to a queen

GALEN O'HANLON makes a splash

DAVID GILMOUR visits a francophile's England

FRANCES WOOD discovers the virtues of rhubarb

What do

DIANA ATHILL · JUDY BENNETT · QUENTIN BLAKE
RONALD BLYTHE · MICHAEL BILLINGTON · TRACY CHEVALIER
ISABEL COLEGATE · CHARLES COLLINGWOOD
CAROL ANN DUFFY · ALAN GARNER · MICHAEL HOLROYD
KATE HUMBLE · KAZUO ISHIGURO · ROBERT MACFARLANE
MATT · SAM MENDES · HELEN MIRREN · MICHAEL MORPURGO
ANDREW MOTION · DERVLA MURPHY · JOHN JULIUS NORWICH
MICHAEL PALIN · LIBBY PURVES · POSY SIMMONDS
ALEXANDER MCCALL SMITH · SUE MACARTNEY SNAPE
and ALAN TITCHMARSH

have in common?

All will be revealed in our Spring 2014 issue.

who fired convention new imagination
challenge & create from their always
who turn their art keep
that bit of us that
makes us greater

Slightly Foxed is delighted to announce the reissue of all
twelve of Ronald Welch's Carey books:

AVAILABLE NOW
Knight Crusade, For the King, The Galleon

March 2014
Captain of Foot

September 2014
Bowman of Crécy, The Hawk

March 2015
Captain of Dragoons

September 2015
Escape from France, Nicholas Carey

March 2016
Mohawk Valley

September 2016
Ensign Carey, Tank Commander

Each title will be published with the original illustrations
in a new limited and numbered cloth-bound edition of
2,000 copies. If you would like to preorder a copy of each title
with the same limited-edition number, please call the office on
020 7033 0258 or email us at all@foxedquarterly.com.